THE BOWERCH
PARISH PAPERS

THE BOWERCHALKE PARISH PAPERS

Collett's Village Newspaper

1878–1924

Rex L. Sawyer

ALAN SUTTON
Published in collaboration with
Wiltshire County Council
Library & Museum Service

ALAN SUTTON PUBLISHING
BRUNSWICK ROAD · GLOUCESTER

British Library Cataloguing in Publication Data

Sawyer, Rex. L.
The Bowerchalke papers: Collett's
Parish village newspaper 1878–1924.
1. Wiltshire. Bowerchalke. Social life,
history.
I. Title
942.3′19

ISBN 0-86299-579-5

Cover illustration: The Revd Edward Collett compiling an issue of the *Parish Papers* – Collection of Mrs Monica Lee

Typesetting and origination by
Alan Sutton Publishing Limited
Printed in Great Britain by
WBC Print Bristol

Contents

Introduction vii

1 Edward Collett 1

2 The *Parish Papers* 12

3 The Village 24

4 The Church 50

5 The Children 73

6 Entertainment 100

7 The First World War 112

8 Widening Horizons 131

Appendix
Ghosts and Legends Concerning Bowerchalke 136

Sources 139

Index 141

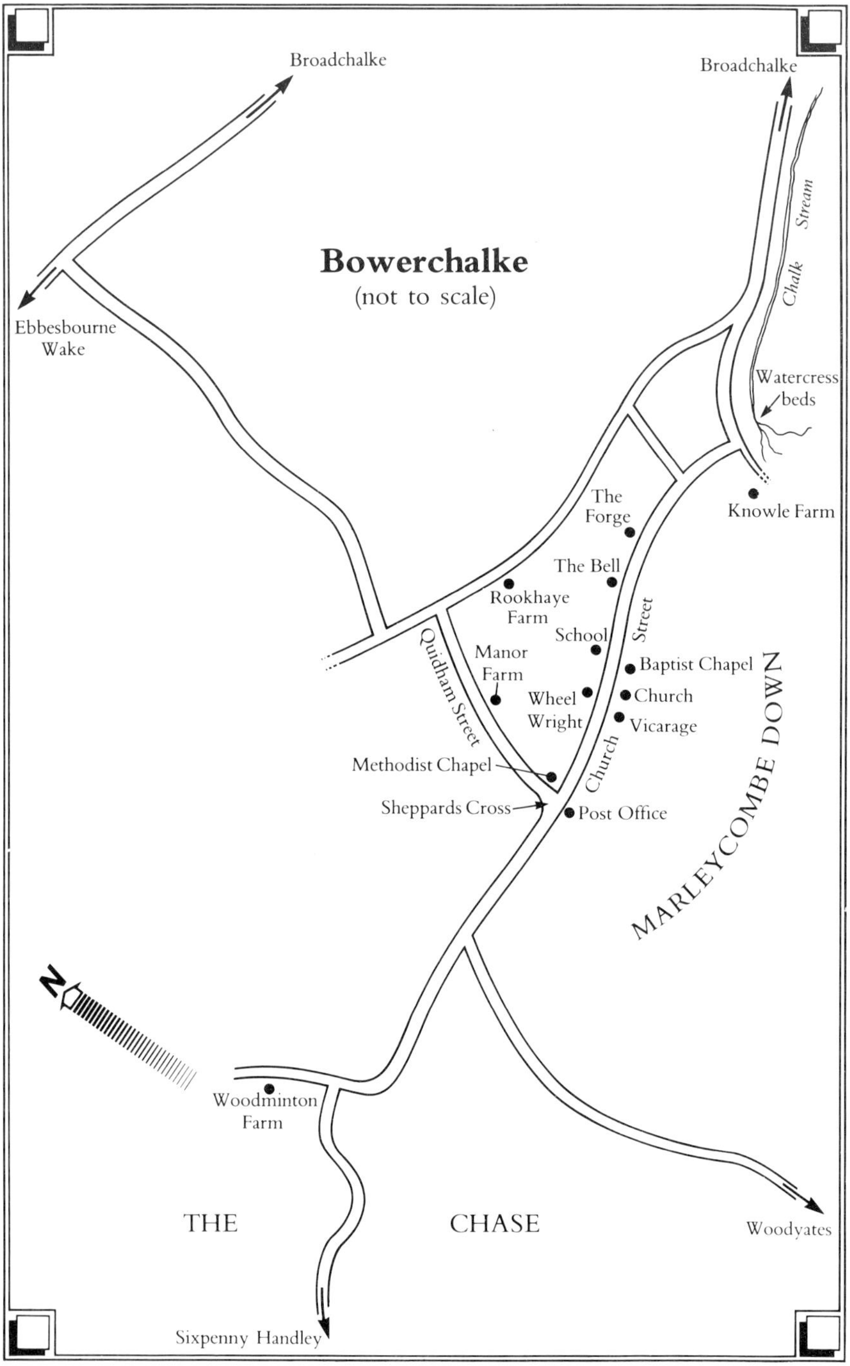

Bowerchalke
(not to scale)
Broadchalke
Broadchalke
Ebbesbourne Wake
Chalk Stream
Watercress beds
Knowle Farm
The Forge
The Bell
Rookhaye Farm
School
Street
Manor Farm
Baptist Chapel
Church
Wheel Wright
Vicarage
Quidham Street
Methodist Chapel
Church
Sheppards Cross
Post Office
MARLEYCOMBE DOWN
N
Woodminton Farm
THE CHASE
Woodyates
Sixpenny Handley

Introduction

It could so easily be missed, this little chalkland village, as many miles from Salisbury as it is from Shaftesbury and once an insignificant settlement on the northern rim of Cranborne Chase. The Ebble Valley road follows a winding course from Salisbury between the ancient downland ridges of the Shaston Drove and the Ox Drove, but at Broadchalke a spur sweeps round the church to run even deeper past succulent cressbeds and heron-haunted trout ponds. Here, at Bowerchalke, I sought a home some ten years ago and found it at The Old Vicarage, a solid structure of grey Chilmark stone, long since vacated by the church.

For the most part the garden was well stocked although it had been latterly laid down for the convenience of busy professional workers, the exception being a stretch of some eight feet at the bottom, age-laden with couch grass, nettles and other long-established weeds, and shunned by the faint-hearted. The south-east corner was dominated by a beautiful, wind-torn cedar, and it was here that I made the discovery that was to spark off many hours of investigation and introduce me to a rather remarkable man. For buried beneath the surface, obviously for many years, was a vast hoard of decayed and decaying objects. Rusting well buckets, tarnished candelabra, ruined photographic plates, obsolete tools and bottles – bottles of all shapes, sizes and colours – gradually gave way to my probing fork accompanied by a chorus of 'oohs' and 'aahs' from a group of little boys who had appeared mysteriously from all corners of the village and were peering curiously over the fence.

Who was responsible for this 'ancient pile'? Why and when was it placed there? These questions led me to the church records, to the Bodleian Library in Oxford, to Suffolk and, finally, back for further investigation of old Salisbury newspapers and the villagers themselves. They introduced me to the Reverend Edward Collett who came to Bowerchalke in 1878, to what the old shire records refer to as 'a meagre dwelling for a curate'. Two years later the living was separated from the dominant church in Broadchalke, two miles further east, and for the next forty-four years until his death Collett continued to serve as its vicar.

Utterly devoted to his parish, Edward Collett was not remarkable for his learning and certainly not for his wealth. He was no travelling diarist like

The Revd Edward Collett

Kilvert, his Wiltshire neighbour, but more akin to Chaucer's Parson, a worker priest with dirty finger nails, finding sufficiency in little things and from the earliest days moulding his life and activities around the village he left only rarely. He showed a concern for all stations of his small society that was perhaps unusual for his time, not just through the official committees and Sunday services, though the latter were extremely important to him, but through the minutiae of everyday existence. These he recorded in his notes, his photographs, his scrapbooks – comically labelled 'This and That' – and, most importantly, through the *Parish Papers*, a weekly newspaper he wrote and printed privately in the vicarage on his own press, selling it at a farthing a copy for the astonishing period of forty years.

An almost complete set of these *Parish Papers* can be viewed at the Bodleian Library in Oxford. Fortunately for me, a more conveniently-placed collection was preserved by Mrs Monica Lee, an elderly villager who had inherited them from her uncle, the vicar's closest friend John Linnell, and had had the good sense to preserve all the papers and many of the photographs. Together they help piece together the activities of a village stripped of rustic sentimentality, but strongly independent of both the influence of the city of Salisbury and the interference of its patron, Lord Pembroke at Wilton.

In preparing this manuscript I have tried to keep two things in view. Firstly, there is the question of balance. Edward Collett is still remembered by a dwindling number of older inhabitants in the Chalke Valley with much affection. There is a great danger, therefore, of producing a eulogy rather than an objective assessment. Not surprisingly, the memories of youth may become distorted by time and it must be remembered that they would have known Collett in his later, perhaps more mellow years.

Collett's own picture of his village must inevitably suffer from a similar lack of objectivity. The *Salisbury Times* reporter who visited him in 1910 in connection with the *Parish Papers* described him as 'combining the functions of proprietor, editor, manager, publisher, printer, sub-editor, chief reporter, machinist, etc.' A remarkable achievement when one considers all his other religious and pastoral activities, but not one calculated to ensure good balanced journalism. As a High Church Anglican, for example, his views and attitudes were somewhat at odds with the strong Dissenter tradition in Bowerchalke and his apparent regard for the schoolmaster Penfound would seem to differ from the view of the Chairman of Managers who wrote in the school log book following Penfound's announcement of his resignation; 'Thank God!'

I was anxious, therefore, to avoid presenting an unbalanced picture and to

The vicarage in 1884. Today the ivy has been replaced by Virginia creeper. To the right the original post office can be seen, but this later blew down during a storm

help counteract this possibility have ranged as widely as possible among the written records of the time in order to put Collett's *Parish Papers* into as broad a context as possible. These sources were the scrapbooks of articles and press cuttings he maintained throughout his years at Bowerchalke, school and church records, local newspapers and other historical papers to which I had access. Where I have used anecdotes or information so helpfully provided by local people I have named the person concerned.

Secondly, there is a very grave danger that villages are becoming (have become?) transformed into dormitories for the retired, the town worker and the holiday-seeker, losing their character, their vitality and much of their authenticity in the process. Collett lived in Bowerchalke during a very important period from this point of view. He unconsciously witnessed and recorded the last final flowering of village life and the beginnings of its decline before the inevitable march of progress led us to the present unfortunate position. I hope that this study may remind us of what is being lost in the process before it is too late.

I should like to place on record my appreciation to Mrs Monica Lee for giving me such generous access to her Edward Collett material and to the many people who have given equally generously of their time in recalling the Bowerchalke of their youth. I should also like to thank my daughter Sara whose own research into the village has been such a valuable aid and my wife Sheila whose typing of the manuscript is so much neater than mine was of the draft! Finally, my appreciation must be expressed to Dr John Chandler, County Archivist for Wiltshire, whose encouragement provided the impetus I needed to complete and give shape to my researches.

Rex L. Sawyer
November 1988

1
Edward Collett

Details of Edward Collett's family background remain very sketchy and for that which is available I am indebted to his only surviving English relative, Mr Harry Collett, a retired farmer now living in Suffolk. During the eighteenth and early nineteenth century the family formed part of the English colony in St Petersburg where their business interests involved cotton. Edward's grandfather, William Wilson, married a Russian girl there in 1814 and produced five daughters. The eldest child, Sophia Eleanor, married John Holmes Collett in 1842 and produced three sons: Augustus, John and Edward. At some stage the family returned to England. Augustus is later recorded as one of several partners in a cotton exchange at Liverpool. Here he lived in comparative prosperity at Sefton Park raising a family of five sons and three daughters. Although the firm is reputed to have gone bankrupt, he obviously remained there as a respected citizen for the Parish Magazine of St Agnes Church, Liverpool, recording his death in September 1911 refers to him as 'a most regular communicant, a staunch friend and a faithful supporter'.

Edward was born in 1847 but nothing is known of his earlier life. Following in the footsteps of his brother John, to whom he remained very close throughout his life, he trained for the ministry at St Bees Theological College in Northumberland and, in 1870, was ordained at Oxford. He then served in six parishes in rapid succession over a period of eight years including the remote Cronk-y-Voddy on the Isle of Man where he tried to improve the cultural atmosphere with a weekly session of *Penny Readings*. His own literary ability and theological thinking were becoming established during this period. In 1874 he published *A Book of Meditations*, and two years later *A Simple Plan of Preparation for Confirmation*; both were to be reviewed favourably in numerous papers and religious periodicals of the time including *The Guardian* of 12 January 1876. From the Isle of Man he went to Silverstone in Northamptonshire where he remained for three years and here he developed something of the vigour, style and institutions he was to favour at Bowerchalke. He also met John Linnell here who, at fourteen years of age, accompanied Collett to Bowerchalke initially with the intention of training for the priesthood but instead he stayed, apart for a

The family of Edward Collett's eldest brother, Augustus, in 1888

short period, to remain friend and confidante to Collett for the rest of the latter's life.

Collett arrived in Bowerchalke, a village largely influenced by Nonconformism, on 30 September 1878 at the age of thirty-one. He was extremely dedicated to his 'High Church' principles and at the height of his powers. At that time Bowerchalke was united with the more prominent parish of Broadchalke under one vicar, although several centuries earlier the two parishes had been independent. In the early part of 1878 the Revd Cecil Gurden Moore accepted the living of the united parishes but was resident at Broadchalke. He found Bowerchalke in the charge of a curate, the Revd Henry Steel, who – through disagreement or choice – promptly resigned. Moore then appointed Edward Collett to be curate in charge of Bowerchalke. It was not to be an auspicious beginning.

Just over a decade earlier in 1866 major restoration had taken place in the church. The ugly high pews, as Collett described them, and the gallery at the west end had been removed and the church enlarged by the addition of the south aisle. Despite this, Collett was not impressed either by the fabric nor by the lack of enthusiasm among his new parishioners. Holy Communion was held only once a month at midday, Evensong was at three and there were no evening services. To his first Celebration came a mere eleven communicants. The chancel was not used and the church, dimly lit by

Edward Collett's brother, the Revd John Collett. He was to finish his ministry in nearby Teffont. Taken in 1885

candles had no vestry so, like his predecessors, he was forced to commence his services directly from his neighbouring vicarage.

With the approach of winter and still struggling to overcome the villagers' innate suspicion of a new incumbent – and a high church one at that – Collett had to contend with not only the resignation of the schoolmistress but the appalling weather that blocked the roads in January for over a week. This was followed by a flood with rapidly thawing snow bursting through the chancel roof and ruining the altar area. Within nine months a second headteacher had resigned and two villagers had walked out of church in protest at his introduction of more elaborate services.

Collett was not a man to compromise, however, and gradually he seems to have gained acceptance of his 'Popish' ways, although between him and the strong representation of Dissenters in the village, there remained a gulf which he rarely attempted to cross. From the beginning he replaced the small girls' choir, (he had an anti-feminist streak which should not be judged in terms of the 1980s), with a choir of 'men and lads' and on Easter Eve 1879 they appeared for the first time in cassocks and surplices occupying the previously redundant chancel stalls at a special service. From the start, Collett's intention had been to stiffen the sinews of his church, to breathe life into an institution that seemed to him to have suffered through being the poorer half of a joint parish. In this he succeeded dramatically, and was rewarded on 1 December 1880, when by order of the Queen in Council, the two parishes were separated and Collett was offered the vacant living.

Isaac Sheppard is a name that appears again and again in the various records of late nineteenth century Bowerchalke. An absentee benefactor, he left the village as a young man to commence business in London, a venture that prospered as he was obviously a wealthy man. He returned each year for the Whitsun Club Day, as well as on other occasions, and continued to show an affectionate interest in the affairs of the village. In one of his *Parish Papers* Edward Collett recalled a significant conversation with him:

> In September 1880, just 30 years ago, a notice appeared in what was then the monthly Parish Paper, saying that a suggestion had been made that a church clock should be put in the tower. The late Mr Isaac Sheppard was prime mover in the matter and we can well remember driving in with him one day to Salisbury and hearing him by way of a joke, propose and get a fellow passenger to second, that a Clock should be got. (This happened just as we were passing the cottage which was then occupied by the late John Humby at Mouse-hole) A concert in aid of the proposed clock was immediately organised by Mr Sheppard and it was given at the Assembly Rooms, Salisbury on Tuesday October 12th, 1880, both in the afternoon and evening.
>
> *Parish Papers* 1 September 1910

The cost of the clock was £95; £50 being donated by Isaac Sheppard and the rest raised by bazaars and donations, the Assembly Rooms concerts having proved a financial disaster. Collett always regarded the clock with great affection. Not surprisingly, perhaps, as it first struck during the midnight service on New Year's Eve 1880, the same day as he was officially instituted as Vicar of Bowerchalke by the Bishop of Salisbury.

From this time on Collett was to stamp his identity with ever-increasing confidence on the life of the village. The eleven communicants at a single Celebration at Easter 1878 had become fifty-four spread over three by 1880 and soon he was extending his services over the whole of the Sabbath with early morning Communion at 4 a.m. on special feast days. It is noteworthy, too, that a bazaar held in December 1879 to raise funds for restoring the bells was held at Broadchalke, whereas in future all functions were to be held in Bowerchalke itself, further proof that the village was beginning to assume a more positive identity, an identity that was unquestionably cemented by the *Parish Papers*.

The *Papers* first appeared in monthly form on 1 July 1880, but weekly from April 1882. Measuring no more than 26 cm by 16 cm or a single-sided sheet of A5 paper they were circulated throughout the village and among friends at a farthing a copy. They were used by Collett, not merely as a

BOWERCHALKE

WEEKLY PARISH PAPER.

"THAT YE MIGHT KNOW OUR AFFAIRS."- EPH. VI. 22.

No. 1673.] WEDNESDAY, JULY 27, 1921. [PRICE ½d.

THIS AND THAT.

THE MOON.—Last Quarter, tomorrow, July 28, at 3·20 A.M.

LIGHTING-UP-TIME.—Today: 8·25, Next Wednesday: 8·14.

SERMON TEXTS.—On Thursday last (by the Rev H. K. HUDSON) "All flesh is as Grass, and all the glory of man as the flower of Grass. The Grass withereth, and the flower thereof falleth away." 1 S. Peter 1, 24. On Sunday last: *M.* "I will always give thanks unto THEE for that THOU hast done." Psalm 52, 10. *E.* "I went into the Field, and, Lo, I have seen, and yet see, that I am not able to express." 2 Esdras 10, 32.

NEXT SUNDAY.—10*th* Sunday after TRINITY, July 31. Church-colour: *Green.* (Commemoration of S. JAMES' Day.) HYMNS. At Mattins: Pro. 411, 570, 413, 237, Rec. 423. At Evensong: Pro. 436, 512, 598, 603, Rec. 397.

HOLY DAY.—Next Monday (August 1) S. PETER'S Deliverance.

SCHOOL HOLIDAYS—have begun this week, and will continue for the next 5 weeks. School will re-open on Monday, August 29.

THE HAY-HARVEST FESTIVAL—began on Sunday-week, and was concluded on Sunday last. In spite of the long spell of very hot weather, the Church was richly decorated with beautiful flowers, in addition to the handsome wreathings of Grasses. We are heartily grateful for all the kind and unselfish efforts of the diligent decorators, who spared no pains in doing their work. The Services were bright and hearty. The Offertories were given towards the expenses of the Sunday-Classes Summer Treat, and amounted to £3. 17. 8. On the Thursday in the week, we had the very welcome privilege of hearing our old friend, the Rev. H. K. HUDSON preach. We thank him most sincerely for his helpful and instructive words.

THE SUMMER-TREAT—took place on Wednesday last, when the Sunday Scholars, and their friends, spent a very happy and enjoyable day at Bournemouth. The Bus, and Mr Beckley's Motor Van, took the happy party away at 10 o'clock, returning at the same hour in the evening, all the better for the beautiful Sea breezes, and the long and pleasant excursion. Everyone, without exception, expressed appreciation of the trip, and the weather was all that could be desired, and we have very much to be grateful for. Mr. Linnell most kindly, and with great success, carried out all arrangements. We thank him most sincerely, and all the many others who helped.

S. P. G. HALF-YEARLY BOXES.—We have to acknowlede with sincerest thanks, the following amounts contained in the Boxes up to the end of June:— 1/11, 2*s*, 2/5, 2/8, 2/9, 2/11½, 3*s*, 3/0½, 3/4, 3/4½, 3/8, 4/1½, 4/2, 5/4, 12/4, 20*s*, 45/7. Total: £6. 2. 8. Of Coins there were 925 (96 Silver, and the rest Copper.)

LAST WEEK—the Parish Paper was not issued, and in the week before, only a small number of them were sent out. We are sorry for this, and hope that our many readers will not think that we had quite forgotten them. So numerous are the various things which call upon one's time, that it is occasionaly needful to leave some out.

Printed at the Vicarage Private Printing Press, Bowerchalke.

Parish Papers Wednesday 27 July 1921

means of announcing church services and allied functions, but for comments on local activities and, sometimes vitriolic, criticisms of village behaviour or national events. Therefore, as a social document of the period 1880–1922 they have a valuable contribution to make.

Collett's involvement in his community is evident at all levels, but it is difficult to gauge to what extent he gave new impetus to older village institutions or created them himself. Either way, his arrival heralded a period of change in which he was prime instigator. In 1881, the first Post Office was opened to replace the wall box, with Josiah Williams as the first Postmaster; Collett was later to press successfully through the *Parish Papers* for a Sunday post and a second delivery of letters. On the other hand, when William Wilkins died a few years later having been Parish Clerk for over twenty-five years, the position became defunct. A Coal Club, subsidised by the better off, was instituted although a Clothing Club already existed and the Pig Club to help augment the limited diet of the cottagers was obviously flourishing with an annual supper for as many as sixty of its members.

Through his broadsheet, and presumably from his pulpit, the new vicar soon made it known that he had little time for politics, finding the whole business of the hustings extremely undignified. He was firmly of the Victorian 'self-help' tradition, believing that the village should look to itself for its own salvation. Nevertheless, he was a man of firm humanitarian principles, not one to hide himself away or to hob-nob with the gentry, preferring to identify with the life of the villagers. Class stratification existed, of course, but the small size of the community, 420 in the 1881 census, and its interdependence as an agricultural community prevented this from becoming too extreme.

The vicarage, with the church, lies centrally along a rise in the road from Broadchalke which provides the main thoroughfare through the village. From here Collett provided a soup kitchen at the price of 1*d.* a pint for the poorest inhabitants and gave away garden produce – strawberry plants, rhubarb, vegetables and flower seeds – to encourage home cultivation and was mainly instrumental in starting the annual Garden Show soon after his arrival. In 1884 he created a library in a downstairs room of the vicarage which was open to all. Although its use was probably limited to the more prosperous and better-educated of local society it continued in use until after his death, the tattered and soiled volumes constantly replenished by kind donations from near and far.

During his ministry at Bowerchalke Edward Collett continued to involve himself with theological writings and dispute. In 1883 he published *God's Choice*, a meditation on the early life of St Mary and *The Parish Priest's Day Book*, highly praised as a practical aid to the daily tasks of a parish priest. His antagonism towards Dissenters was expressed quite waspishly on occasions in the *Parish Papers* and his basic theological differences with them were given their first public airing at a quite remarkable conference over which he presided on 6 March 1882. The conference was sparked off by a lecture on the church given by the schoolmaster, Mr Kendall. At that meeting some of the Dissenters present challenged certain points raised and requested an opportunity for further discussion. This was agreed and both sides must have mustered their forces with great enthusiasm for we are told that about 500 members of the Anglican and Baptist denominations squeezed into a barn belonging to Shrewsbury Harding, a farmer in Quidham Street, the subject of debate being Baptism.

A full account of the conference was published in the local papers of the time and subsequently taken up by *The Guardian* of 22 March 1882 which reported that a series of speeches were given by specially selected speakers and proceeded for over four hours. The main points of contention appear to have been whether total immersion as practised by the Baptists or the 'sprinkling of Infants' had greater biblical authority, and the question of what age baptism should take place. Revd Short from Salisbury and Revd Collier from Downton were the main Baptist speakers but the eminence of the main Anglican members, Earl Nelson, who spoke for an hour and a quarter and E.B. Ottley, Principal of Salisbury Theological College, is an indication of Collett's standing among his church brethren. Despite cries of 'Popery' when Collett made his opening remarks and criticisms of the Church of England as 'the Church of bloody Jeffery and Bonner', the occasion seems to have passed off comparatively peacefully.

Sarah Stone – she came to Bowerchalke with the vicar in 1878 from his previous parish in Silverstone. Taken in 1884

Bad behaviour among young people is not confined to the twentieth century, nor to urban areas alone. The lack of amenities leading to idleness and thence to mischief was a problem that Collett mentioned frequently in his *Papers*:

> The very rough and insolent conduct of some of the 'Big Boys' (who imagine themselves men), has become so unbearable, reflecting also great discredit upon their parents, that steps are now being taken to punish, with utmost rigour, all those who by collecting at the street corners, by using bad language, or by laughing at, and otherwise insulting passers by are guilty of misdemeanour; or who commit a trespass by intruding themselves either into Churchyard or School yard or who damage, or disfigure the Churchyard or other walls by marking or writing on them. Mr Collett is now in correspondence with the Superintendent of Police on the subject.
>
> *Parish Papers* 10 March 1883

The nearest policeman, Sgt. Cruse, was stationed at Broadchalke and would have had difficulty in being on hand on such occasions, but things had reached such a pitch by March 1883 that it was decided to have a public meeting in the schoolroom of all householders and other interested parties to decide what could be done. Superintendent Stevens of the Salisbury Police was present as well as Sgt Cruse to give weight to the proceedings. As a result of the meeting resolutions were agreed and, at the suggestion of Superintendent Stevens, these were printed and then posted at various points in the village. This document outlined the main offences objected to and promised to use all lawful means to suppress them. It called on the particular attention of parents to care for their children properly and not allow them to loiter about the village in idleness. It is doubtful whether this had any long-term effect as the *Parish Papers* continued to complain of misdemeanours. In 1886 the *Salisbury Journal* reported that one boy from Bowerchalke had been sent to a reformatory and several other cases over the years came before the Salisbury magistrates whose sentences were somewhat harsher than those of today.

An incident in 1888 led to one of the periodic differences of opinion between Collett and the Dissenters. The lamp by the Methodist Chapel, provided by Isaac Sheppard eight years earlier, had been systematically vandalised until only the stem was left. In the *Parish Paper* Collett criticised those who caused the damage since it meant to benefit them and Henry Butler, on behalf of his Wesleyan congregation, took exception to this thinking he was referring to them. Collett was led to a grudging apology and the lamp, refurbished by Isaac Sheppard, was placed instead at the entrance to the school yard.

Collett was the first to admit that domestic conditions, cramped and unhealthy with no outlets for the natural buoyancy of young people, often

John Linnell in 1885. He came to Bowerchalke with Edward Collett from Silverstone, and played a prominent part in most village activities

drove them onto the streets in sheer desperation. Despite the perennial problems and his sternness when the occasion demanded, Collett was extremely fond of children; a large part of his activities in one way or another was concerned with them. There is no doubt that the development of his very successful church choir, the Sunday school and its special treats, (summer and winter), the continuous village entertainments he encouraged, his involvement in the National School and his encouragement of village clubs and activities over the years did much to reduce the problems of boredom by providing many more positive outlets for energy than appear to have existed before.

Apart from the village children, his genuine regard for young people is shown through his life-long efforts on behalf of the 'Waifs and Strays', forerunner of the modern Church of England Children's Society. Through his instigation a home, St Bartholomew's, was started for them and following the death of Miss Wilkins who ran it, he persuaded some of the villagers to have the children in their own homes. Letters from these young people to him were reported in the *Parish Papers* through the years as they continued their careers in this country and abroad. There were regular parties of children from the East End of London too, who came down for holidays during the summer travelling by train to Salisbury and thence by the carrier's van to Bowerchalke to stay in the homes of villagers. Tea and games on the vicarage lawn were always a feature of their stay.

Part of his evident success with young children would have been due to his sense of humour. Despite his grim and sometimes bigoted observations on certain aspects of society, the *Papers* show much evidence of a delightful ability to see the funny side of village life and to laugh at the eccentricities he saw in others as well as himself; indeed, in a village entertainment in 1903, a poem criticising his 'missionary activities and ritualism' while at his previous parish on the Isle of Man was read as part of the programme. Some of his most wicked humour was reserved for his old friend the village clock which received a teasing every time it went wrong:

> The church clock has recently been more or less unreliable as to exact time and has apparently been suffering from an attack of (mechanical) Influenza, which has exhibited itself in a variety of ways more pleasing to itself than to the public in general! When it came to striking as many strokes as it felt inclined to, instead of speaking the truth, we thought it was only right to silence it altogether. Eventually we had to call in the 'doctor' and on Monday last Mr Silverthorne of Salisbury and his assistant 'surgeon' performed a series of delicate internal operations with great success. All the 'insides' were taken out and cleaned, an insult which the poor clock sulkily resented by holding its hands over its face at the same hour all through the day. However, so soon as everything was put right again, like human beings are wont to do, it recovered its temper and at five o'clock began to work and strike and has continued 'amiable' ever since.
>
> *Parish Papers* 4 January 1900

Collett's humour also reflects for us his love and observation of animal and bird life. His scrapbooks, for example, contained a colleague's description of his kittens: 'Tom has a black coat, white waistcoat and stockings and whiskers; Harriet is a tabby, with white pinafore and whiskers.' Then there is this wonderful description of the intricate fluting of the thrush:

> Swank, swank, swank, swank, swank. Get your beak clipped, get your beak clipped, get your beak clipped. Tut, tut, tut, tut, tut. Cheese it do, cheese it do, cheese it do. Naughty, naughty, naughty, naughty. Pip-pip, pip-pip, pip-pip. She's a peach, peach, peach, peach, peach, PEACH. For you to eat? for you to eat? for you to eat? I *don't* think. I *don't* think. I *don't* think. Cool cheek Cool cheek Cool cheek. I fill the bill, I'm it, I fill the bill, I'm it, I fill the bill, I'm it. Swank, swank, swank, swank! (and so on).
>
> *Parish Papers* 11 June 1913

On the other hand, he wrote with horror at the terrible agony caused by the thoughtless adoption of the gin trap and placed a petition for signatures in the church porch following his sermon on vivisection. To encourage the children's innate fondness for animals he gave active support to a branch of the 'Band of Mercy', a weekly winter meeting under the patronage of Miss

Church St., Bowerchalke in 1884

Aldwyckle, a tall and imposing lady of independent means with eyes of differing colours.

In 1906, Collett wrote *Narrow Windows*, a booklet described as 'short and very beautiful meditations in Lent'; five years later he published *An Excellent Mystery*, three marriage addresses in a daintily-bound little volume. These he used, 'in place of the somewhat antiquated and stilted homily provided in the Prayer Book', and varied according to whether he was addressing regular, occasional or non-communicants. These were his only assays into print during his later years apart from the occasional letters to the local press under such pseudonyms as 'Pecksniff', or 'Pen and Ink'. All his energies, outside of his normal pastoral pursuits, went into the *Parish Papers* which catalogued the events of his village over nearly half a century and provide a more lasting memorial than anything else he wrote.

2
The Parish Papers

Described by the *Daily Chronicle* of 20 September 1911 as 'the smallest paper with comparatively the biggest circulation in the world' and by the *Salisbury Times* as 'a remarkable record in village journalism', the *Parish Paper* was probably unique in its character, its length of survival and its price. As a means of crossing the social, economic and religious boundaries and drawing the village together it was highly successful and it provided a record of village activities over forty years. History, of course, is littered with parish newspapers, magazines or weekly letters, but none have stayed the course for anything like so long or complete a session. Moreover, starting with a circulation of eighty-five, it grew to over four hundred copies weekly, half of which helped bind the village to its friends and family – many of them serving soldiers or homesick colonial emigrants – by being sent in monthly instalments, often subsidised by Collett's meagre income, to Canada, India, New Zealand, Australia, Africa and the United States, as well as to every English county except two.

Why he conceived the idea is not known. There is no evidence that he did anything similar in his previous parishes. Neither does he record where he obtained his printing press. Photographs in the *Daily Mirror* of 14 January 1913 show him setting up the type in a small room in the vicarage by the light of an oil lamp. By this time he was well into his sixties and the photographs show him as a sturdy man, slightly bent, with close-cropped hair and a fringe of white beard. He is dressed, as always, in a black cassock buttoned to his clerical collar and girded with a heavy sash, his enormous hands, a feature of all the Colletts, seeming to dwarf the tiny print.

As the *Salisbury Times* pointed out in its long article of 1910, it may seem an easy thing to churn out a small parish newspaper and to underestimate the physical and mental effort required over such a sustained period. Apart from the actual writing, the printing processes were slow; each edition entailed many hours of tedious labour in type-setting alone, to say nothing of the printing. There was then the slow business of cleaning and methodically putting the type back in its cases ready to be picked up again for the following week's edition. Despite this, I cannot remember finding a single mistake. Then there were the problems of distribution. Fred Penny,

BOWERCHALKE

WEEKLY PARISH PAPER.

"THAT YE MIGHT KNOW OUR AFFAIRS."- EPH. VI. 22.

No. 1133.] THURSDAY, DECEMBER 29, 1910. [PRICE ½d.

HOLY BAPTISM.—DIMMER.—On Thursday last, Dec. 22, MARGARET LOTTIE MAY, infant-daughter of Sidney & Jessie Dimmer.

HOLY MATRIMONY.—ANDREWS - VINCENT.—On Monday last, December 26 (S. Stephen's Day) John Alfred Andrews, of Midsomer Norton (Somt) to Frances Mary Vincent, of this parish.

DEATH.—GEAR.—At 20 Farley Road, Salisbury, on Friday last, December 23, James Gear, formerly of Bowerchalke, aged 80.

THIS AND THAT.

THE MOON.—New Moon, next Saturday, Dec. 31, at 4·21 P.M.

LIGHTING-UP-TIME.—Today : 4·56. Next Thursday : 5·3.

SERMON TEXTS.—Last Sunday : *M.* "HE sent HIS WORD, and healed them, and they were saved." Psalm cvii, 20. *E.* "In the likeness of sinful flesh, and for sin." Romans viii, 3.

NEXT SUNDAY.—*CHRISTMAS Octave*, January 1, 1911. Festival of the Circumcision of CHRIST.—Church-colour : *White.* New Year's Day. At Mattins : HYMNS. Pro.77, 78, 64, 75, Rec.327. At Evensong : Pro.78, 66, 65, 77, Rec.61.

THE RAILWAY DISASTER—which occurred to the Scotch Express on Christmas Eve, was very awful. We shall have intercession next Sunday at Celebration, for the Souls of those who were killed, and that the consolation of GOD may be granted to those who mourn.

HOLY DAYS.—[See Prayer-Book Calendar.]—Next Saturday (31) S. Sylvester Bishop. A.D 335. Next Sunday (Jan. 1) Festival of the Circumcision of our LORD. Church-colour : *White.*

THE REV. JOHN COLLETT—tells us he is regaining strength by slow degrees, and that his Doctor is satisfied with his progress. He can now manage to walk a little without the help of a stick. This news encourages us to hope that perfect recovery is near at hand.

ON CHRISTMAS DAY—the congregations were very good, and there were 57 Communicants. We are much encouraged. Thanks to the ever thoughtful kindness of Miss Freeth, we did not lack Flowers for the decorations, and we also received a box of beautiful Chrysanthemums from Miss Constance Wright (Devon). The Offertories were for the Waifs and Strays Society, and amounted to £1. 9. 2.

THE SCHOOL—will re-open after the holidays, on Monday next.

S.P.G. BOXES—will be collected on Monday next, January 2. We sincerely hope that very good care has been taken during the last six months, that the contributions have been regular and willing. Each offering ought always to be accompanied by a silent little prayer (such as, 'Take this O GOD, and bless it.') By so doing we are making a Box to be a blessing to ourselves and to our homes.

THE CHILDREN—very much appreciated the Lantern Pictures last Thursday afternoon, although it was impossible to sufficiently darken the room so as to see them at their best. It was so very kind of Mr. Sparrowe to come over from Handley, in spite of rough weather and flooded roads. But we feel quite sure that in his unselfish pleasure of entertaining the youngsters, he forgot his own discomforts. We thank him most heartily, and Miss Aldwinckle also for gift of Buns.

TWO SOCIALS—have been held in the Schoolroom this week, under the excellent management of Mr. Linnell, and to the great enjoyment of the guests. And tonight there is to be a Supper (very kindly given by Miss Wood) for the Choir-men. So we are having a merry time this holiday-week, while we are getting ready for the New Year.

Printed at the Vicarage Private Printing Press, Bowerchalke.

still living in the village, remembers assisting with this task and being known by Collett as the BWPPB – the Bowerchalke Weekly Parish Paper Boy. Finally, there was the onerous task of arranging the monthly payment. A farthing a week does not seem much but some, he grumbled, were twelve to eighteen months in arrears. Human nature being what it is, a few others delayed payment and then disputed that they owed anything at all or else pretended that they had not received their copy. To counteract this he later adopted the practice of enclosing these people's edition's in a paper wrapper bearing on it the amount due.

The origins of the *Parish Papers* lay in a monthly magazine printed elsewhere and first issued in July 1880 with a four-page local insert which Collett added. Unfortunately, copies of these no longer exist. At the beginning of 1882 this was discontinued in favour of a magazine which actually printed the local material for him in London. Not surprisingly the experiment proved to be too expensive and in March of that year the first edition of the *Weekly Parish News*, as it was then named, was published on the vicarage private printing press with a modest circulation of copies. It then continued with remarkably few hiccoughs until April 1922.

To the incurious eye, the *Parish Papers* may seem somewhat dull. Beneath the title, displayed in large black lettering, there lies a motto he retained throughout – 'That ye may know our affairs', a quotation from Ephesians, Chapter 6. The contents of each edition may be roughly divided into several categories: there was, of course, a list of church services and special saints days for the coming week preceded by an 'editorial' often of a religious nature linked with this section was a record of births, marriages and deaths that had taken place there was then an abundance of local information such as the particular phase of the moon and lighting-up time – throughout this period bicycles were a major form of transport. Within this category might come items of less immediate concern such as details from past church records or the heights of the surrounding downs – Collett had a passion for such details. Occasionally he would include games for the children giving a small prize, for example, to the first to discover the correct number of a certain letter in that week's edition.

A third category of information, the accounts of local events or incidents concerning the villagers themselves, is of particular interest to local historians. Nothing escaped his attention, from the national celebrations of royal events to the movement of labourers at the Michaelmas Flitchings. Finally, there were the observations and criticisms that Collett himself made on the state of affairs both locally and nationally. Here he showed neither fear nor favour, seeming just as ready to take the tenant farmers to task for not giving a lead in the Flower Show arrangements as to bring Lord Pembroke's attention to the poor state of sanitation in Quidham Street. Nor, as we have seen, was he above using the *Parish Papers* as a vehicle of

The Bell Inn, Bowerchalke, recently converted into a private residence

social control concerning village behaviour. In 1892 he even printed four extra copies of one edition with an added sentence: 'Peter Williams is such a lazy boy, that he could not learn his Collect last Sunday. For shame Peter!'

By the beginning of the new century, the *Parish Papers* were beginning to become known outside the immediate area. 1901 saw the first reference to it in the *Salisbury Times*, the reporter describing it rather slightingly as 'a High Church paper of low price' and speculating on whether Collett's custom of publishing the banns of marriage might not lead to legal wrangles should either party decide to back down. In 1906, however, it was mentioned as far away as Hull. 'Where is Bowerchalke?' asked the editor of the *Hull Daily Mail*, 'I never heard of the place before until yesterday when I got a copy of the weekly parish paper . . . it appears to have had an extended career as it has got up to No 915 . . . the vicarage private press has also a solitary advertisement. It does not yet boast of cyclopaedias of literature but announces that curly green cabbage plants may be had at 3*d*. per hundred!' Collett was very puzzled by this entry when he received a copy from the kindly editor; as far as he knew there were no subscribers to his paper in that far corner of Yorkshire. In 1907, the *Daily Express* noted its existence as a much senior rival to a farthing newspaper started by the vicar of East Dulwich to combat the semi-heathenism of South London.

Mr and Mrs Barden, 22 August 1889

On 7 February 1908 the *Parish Paper* celebrated its one thousandth edition and Collett printed it on pink-tinted paper, an event noted in the *Salisbury Mirror* and the *Western Gazette*. In this edition Collett thanked God for sparing him through the many years it had taken to produce one thousand copies, while feeling sure it had been a help to some and a bond to many. Its circulation had by then risen to 250, over 100 of which were parcelled up in monthly instalments and sent abroad. In the following year, however, the vicar had a breakdown and for three months the *Parish Papers* were not published, although with the exception of two Sundays he struggled on with his church commitments. However, by January 1910 he was back at the press but stated: 'With reference to the *Parish Paper* it will be issued as far as possible once a week but we cannot make any definite promise as it depends on how the vicar's hand may be able to get on with the work of type-setting.'

He appears to have made a good recovery for the weekly editions continue with but a short break in March. On 27 May of that year the *Salisbury Times* published a very long and glowing article that proved something of a watershed for the *Paper's* popularity:

> The parish of Bowerchalke, isolated as it is ten miles from Salisbury, never the less provides the world of letters, and the world at large with a unique effort in local journalism and has done for many a year past. . . .

Having summarised the history of the paper which the reporter laughingly described as 'having the largest circulation in Bowerchalke', he referred to Collett as combining in his personality all the arduous functions of 'proprietor, editor, manager, publisher, printer, sub-editor, chief reporter, machinist, etc. of this truly remarkable production'. During his visit to Bowerchalke vicarage the reporter had examined the files and discussed with the sprightly old vicar important events in the village's history as depicted there. He quoted liberally from Collett's humorous writing on the eccentricities of the village clock and in more serious vein mentioned that the Bodleian Library, Oxford had written to Collett requesting a complete file of the *Parish Papers*. As complete a selection as possible had been forwarded and another name added to Collett's list of future subscribers.

To Collett's astonishment this article in the *Salisbury Times* was taken up by the national press and reported widely:

> London has with great condescension and kindness extended its favourable notice to our *Parish Paper*. In consequence of the very kindly article which recently appeared in the *Salisbury Times* a short paragraph was inserted in most of the London daily papers on Wednesday June 15th. The weekly followed suit both in town and country and we have in consequence received no end of letters and enquiries and requests for copies. We are more than grateful to the Press for the publicity given to our tiny Paper whose only distinction lies in the fact that it is smaller and of less importance than any other.
>
> *Parish Papers* 23 June 1910

For one brief moment Bowerchalke found itself, a remote country village, picked up and examined under the national microscope as something of a curiosity possessing 'the smallest newspaper with comparatively the biggest circulation in the world', 100 per cent according to the *Daily Chronicle*. Most papers merely quoted from the original *Salisbury Times* article but there had been sufficient stir for that same newspaper to refer to it again two months later as 'unique in its price and the length of its history' and to reproduce a facsimile of the *Parish Paper* of 23 June.

The correspondence that arrived at the vicarage as a result of this publicity certainly enlivened Collett's life:

> One correspondent who by his kindness to animals has won the name of the Donkeys Friend, tells us he was born at Harnham. A telepathist at Birmingham writes pleasantly mysterious letters which puzzle us. A brother-priest who also goes in for printing asks for our Paper and kindly sends us his.

Bowerchalke policemen, 1890. The behaviour of local youngsters who gathered on street corners was a cause for concern at this time

> Several hope to visit Bowerchalke; a lady sends us the manuscript of a long Novel for publication! One writes from Yorkshire that he understands we deal in farthings and he would deem it a favour if we could supply him with 5*s*. worth! A post card comes from Leeds as follows: 'Sir, I want you to send me old copeys of your farthing paper. I might ad to it interest.' These are only a few of the many communications we have received during the last fortnight.
>
> *Parish Papers* 30 June 1910

He also seems to have learnt some of the more esoteric aspects of his small art. Among the curious papers brought to his attention was *The Regal* which was apparently printed on thin sheets of dough, with non-poisonous ink so that it could be eaten as well as read. Another brought to his notice, the *Luminaria*, was printed in an ink containing phosphorus so that its contents could be read in the dark. The *Mouchoir*, printed on thin Japanese paper, had appeared in Paris for a few years and could be used as a pocket handkerchief as well as a news-sheet, while a similar one in India, made in linen, could be returned to the publisher, washed and re-issued the following week!

The thirtieth birthday of the *Parish Paper* and its 1,200th edition was printed on 15 April 1912. Collett again expressed his gratitude that he had been spared to continue it for so long feeling sure that, in spite of its insignificance, it had been 'a real bond of union between us and our friends both at home and abroad.' A few months earlier, for example, he had referred to Jack Morris, a youngster from the village who had emigrated to Canada and was employed by the Canadian Pacific Railway. His brother Sidney had a homestead 1,600 miles further west and was doing well. Both expressed great pleasure at receiving the *Parish Papers* with all their news from home. In 1915 came a letter from Australia sent by a lady who thanked him for the pleasant memories it conjured up of the dear little village of her youth.

Conversely, the news the paper conveyed could be of even more than usual immediacy as is shown by an amusing incident recalled by Fred Penny. In 1891 the wife of Henry Foyle, who lived lower down the village in the Terrace Cottages, gave birth to their first child. The Foyle family underpinned the village economy as wheelwrights, undertakers and agricultural engineers, working from a yard almost opposite the vicarage. When news of the birth was conveyed to the vicar he was working on a fresh edition of the *Parish Paper* in his upper room. He immediately added this to his copy and sent a boy with it over to the yard where Henry Foyle, a carpenter, was able to read the news of his first son which had occurred just down the road!

Isaac Habgood in 1888. He was later to become village postmaster, where he remained until his death aged eighty-eight when he was the oldest postmaster in England

From 1915 a new phase began, reported more fully in a later chapter, when the *Paper* echoed the sadness descending on Bowerchalke with news trickling in of harsh conditions, injuries and deaths as the First World War took its toll, a catalogue repeated in every town and tiny hamlet across the nation. The village must have felt a particular gratitude to Collett at this time as letters to parishioners from their sons in France, Gibraltar, Egypt, Salonica and other foreign outposts expressed thanks for the 'whiff of dear old home' that the *Parish Papers* brought to them. In no case would that have been more true than that of Percy George, brought up in the home for Waifs and Strays, who was captured in 1914 and spent the entire war as a prisoner. The *Parish Papers*, sometimes supplemented by gifts from the village, was a lifeline to him helping to keep him going often under the most appalling conditions.

As the war progressed, Collett's production problems grew. He must have realised that his *Parish Paper* was providing a much needed boost to morale, but paper was becoming increasingly scarce and expensive, a very severe strain on his meagre resources. In January 1918 he wrote, 'It is more than likely that we shall be obliged to lessen the size of our paper before long. We hope that it will not become necessary to discontinue it although it is now and has been for a very long time past run at a considerable loss.' Somehow he managed to struggle on through the ensuing months of the war but the problems were obviously increasing. On 11 September he wrote:

> We have for a considerable time been in doubt as to whether it will not be wise to stop issuing our little paper. Owing to the enormous increase in the price of paper it has been run at a dead loss for a long time past. There are several methods by which this might be lessened such as: 1. making it half its present size, 2. issuing it only once a fortnight, 3. stopping all copies sent by post. But we should much prefer to withdraw it altogether than to adopt any of these plans. We merely mention the matter now so that our many kind friends and readers may be prepared for any possible developments in the near future of the Parish Paper. But we have no wish to discontinue its publication if it can be avoided.
>
> *Parish Papers* 11 September 1918

Fortunately, he did not have to adopt any of these alternatives although how he managed to finance it is not known. Those who remember him speak of him as an enormously generous man and doubtless he dug deeper into his pockets, subsidised, perhaps, by a few kind benefactors. His 'war efforts' and obvious self-sacrifice did not go unnoticed, however, and not long after the conclusion of the war he felt moved to write:

> The vicar wishes most gratefully to acknowledge innumerable letters from kind readers of the Parish Paper both at home and in distant places in England

Misselfore, showing the pond where droves of sheep were watered on their way to Wilton Sheep Fair

> and abroad all generously expressing true appreciation. He cannot sufficiently thank his correspondents and is so sorry that in many cases he has not yet had time to reply.
>
> *Parish Papers* 15 January 1919

Nevertheless, the strain of the war years and forty-one years of ministering to his parish had taken its toll. In February 1919 he apologised that the *Parish Paper* was so late but he had been far from well. In the following week he confessed that he was having difficulty in coping but after 1,500 more or less regular editions he hoped to be excused as 'the setting up of type and the printing of very nearly 400 copies every week does not leave very much time for other necessary work. . . . We shall try our very best to continue the paper to the end.' Yet again on the 21 February: 'The vicar feels that he needs a little rest and especially so as he is not very well'.

This might well have been the end but three weeks later the *Parish Papers* had started up again as vigorously as ever with references to all the slowly reviving village activities after the austerity of war and in May there were thanks from Walter McTier who was still receiving his copy in British Columbia. On 7 January 1921 in another long article the *Salisbury Times* reported that the Bowerchalke *Parish Paper* was still going as strongly as ever just having produced its 1,647th edition. The old clock, it notes, was still giving trouble having struck ten when it should have struck three, a form of increased output which the editor felt would please Mr Lloyd George even if it perplexed Bowerchalke.

However, 1921 saw several breaks in continuity, with the vicar asking pardon for the inconvenience after so many years of regular supply. Apart from illness Collett received another blow when the cost of postage was raised. By this time, out of a circulation of 400 per week, 170 were kept back and sent weekly (at home), and monthly (abroad), through the Post Office. The previous ½*d.* rate had cost him £4 5*s.* 0*d.* annually; this would now be doubled. As Collett remarked, 'It seems unreasonable to be charged 1*d.* to convey a ¼*d.* paper.' All editions sent away now had to go monthly and even this must have been a strain.

The last copy appeared on 12 April 1922 with no explanation for its discontinuance, but it seems certain that the vicar's increasingly poor health would have been the prime cause. He died on 7 May 1924 at which point his lifelong friend John Linnell collected together his printing tools and ink bottles burying them at the end of the garden with many other mementos of his existence. The printing press, I am told, lay mouldering in a field before eventually being buried with an old Model T Ford by the side of the road.

Outside Bowerchalke vicarage – the old gate

BOWERCHALKE

WEEKLY PARISH PAPER.

"THAT YE MIGHT KNOW OUR AFFAIRS" EPH. VI. 22.

No. 1518.] WEDNESDAY, JUNE 19, 1918. [PRICE ½d.

THIS AND THAT.

THE MOON.—Full Moon, next Monday, June 24, at 11·38 P.M.

LIGHTING-UP-TIME.—Today · 9·48. Next Wednesday: 9·49.

SERMON TEXTS—On Sunday last: *M.* "Let us come before HIS Presence with thanksgiving." Psalm 95, 2. *E.* "Having land, sold it, and brought the money, and laid it at the Apostles feet." Act 4, 37.

NEXT SUNDAY.—*4th. Sunday after Trinity*, June 23. (Eve of the Nativity of S. JOHN the Forerunner). Church-colour: *Green* at Mattins, *White* at Evensong. HYMNS. At Mattins: Pro.467, 493, 474, 570, Rec.403. At Evensong: Pro.219, 206, 323, 234, Rec.244.

HOLY DAYS.—[See Prayer-Book Calendar.] Tomorrow (20*th*) S. Edward, King & Martyr, A.D 982. Next Monday (24*th*) Nativity of S. JOHN the Forerunner. Church-colour: *White.*

THE 24TH BIRTHDAY—of His Royal Highness EDWARD, PRINCE OF WALES, takes place on Sunday next, June 23.

THE SCHOOL—will re-open, after the Hay-Harvest Holidays, next Monday morning, June 24.

OUR BISHOP—with his usual great sympathy, has written to the Vicar, in reference to the lamented death of Mr. Butler's Son (the notice of which he read in the Parish Paper). He writes as follows: "I do not remember being told about young Butler's death. Will you tell the parents how grieved I am for them, and how sorry I did not know." His Lordship's kindness is very gratefully appreciated.

SOCIAL REFORM.—At the Meeting which was held on Thursday last, the Rev. Francis Raikes explained the objects and intentions aimed at by the movement he represented. He suggested that in every parish a small Committee should be elected to help forward the work. With that intention a Meeting of Parishioners will be held in the School-room, on Friday evening next, at 7·30. [We understand that there is also to be a Meeting of the Social Reform Council in the Mission Room, Bishopstone, next Thursday evening, at 7·30.]

THE MEMORIAL TABLET—to Bert Bracher, must now be seen to, and we hope that the many friends from whom he has been parted for a while, and who have his companionship in affectionate remembrance, will gladly and lovingly do their best to perpetuate his memory, by placing a worthy record of his faithful service in the Choir. Without any unnecessary delay, we ask all who wish to contribute to the cost of the Brass Tablet, to be so kind as to let us know what they can contribute. We have (as previously stated) received £1, from an anonymous friend, and since then 2*s* from someone else. It will of course depend upon the total amount promised, as to the kind of Tablet we may be able to secure. But we feel sure of hearty support.

FOUND—in the Churchyard, between the Church and Vicarage, a small Gold BROOCH. Apply to Mr. Linnell, Vicarage.

FOUND—on the road between East Chase & Woodyates, a Carriage-WHIP. Apply to Mr. James Trowbridge.

Printed at the Vicarage Private Printing Press, Bowerchalke.

3
The Village

It is interesting to note when looking at the photographs Collett took in the 1880s how little the village appears to have changed in over a hundred years. The road westwards from Broadchalke follows the Chalke Stream, a tributary of the Ebble. It was of this that Aubrey, the Wiltshire historian, wrote in the mid-seventeenth century:

> The rivulet that gives the name to Chalke-bourne and running through Chalke, rises at a place called Naule, (Knowle) belonging to the farme of Broadchalke, where are a great many springs that issue out of the chalke ground. It makes a kind of lake of the quantity of about 3 acres. There are not better trouts (two foot long) in the kingdom of England than here; I was thinking to have made a trout pond of it. The water of this streame washes

Haymaking in Church field. The photograph was taken from the vicarage in 1885

> well and is good for brewing. I did put in a crawfish but they would not live here: the water is too cold for them. This river water is so acrimonious that strange horses when they are watered here will snuff and snort, and cannot well drinke of it till they have been for sometime used to it. Methinks this water should bee admirably good for whitening clothes for cloathiers because it is impregnated so much with nitre, which is abstersive.

Aubrey's intentions are uncannily reflected in the modern day usage, a trout farm has now replaced the once flourishing cressbeds.

At Mead End the stream veers away from the road to disappear beneath Knowle Hill from the top of which, in sheep-covered pastures, the Williamson graves look down on the rich arable land they once farmed. At Applespill Bridge, a tiny lane branches around the northern edge of the village to the aptly named Rookhaye, a chilly Victorian farmhouse where the Methodist, Henry Butler, farmed and raised his large family. The broader village road continues on, however, the main artery of activity, past the church, Sheppards Cross, Misselfore, Castle, to Woodminton where it leaves the village passing through the steep downs to Sixpenny Handley. Mid-way along, at Sheppards Cross, it branches right by the one remaining shop into Quidham Street before winding northwards to rejoin the main valley road from Broadchalke to Ebbesbourne Wake. Further on at Misselfore, is a further junction, this time southwards across the downs to East Chase Farm, and onwards to Woodyates where it joins the ancient Blandford to Salisbury road.

This simple framework is shown very clearly on a map produced by John Andres in 1773 and probably existed centuries before then although in Norman times Bowerchalke was still incomplete as a parish. Bowles, writing in 1829, suggested that it was probably part of the seven and a half hides of land belonging to Richard Poingiant surveyed in the Domesday Book under the title of 'Chelche'. Its name of Bower, or Burghe, Chalk is believed to have derived from the family of Atte Burghe and certainly in 1456 a John Atte Burghe died in possession of land in this parish. At some stage it joined the vast estates of the Abbesses of Wilton remaining with them until the Dissolution when a significant part came, through William Herbert, to the Earls of Pembroke who parcelled out portions to freeholders for an annual rent.

At this period, Bowerchalke was still part of the 'outer ring' of Cranborne Chase and thus subject to the Lord Warden, an official appointed by the ruling monarch or his representative. Under him were various minor officials including woodwards who were responsible for their section of the Chase. They had to report twice-yearly to the Chase Court in connection with infringements of Chase Law, deer slaying, for example, or the illicit grazing of sheep. The woodward at Bowerchalke is mentioned in this

Binghams Farmhouse in 1885. It remains virtually unchanged today

Woodminton Farm in 1885. The farmer, Charles Elliott, had fir trees planted around the house to stop his workers catching glimpses of his daughters undressing

connection by a keeper from Handley in a deposition before the court in 1594.

In 1618, when the Ebble farmers were becoming increasingly incensed by the intrusions of the Chase deer on their crops, one observer wrote; 'if the deer of the Chase should feed out in the cornfields, meadows and pastures of Bowerchalke without restraint, the inhabitants and tenants there would be undone.' This resentment against the harsh Chase laws, which also prevented them tilling the woodland and commons in a way they would have liked, probably explains the complacent attitude that existed towards deer slaying, a crime practised even by the gentry. Harry Goode, a member of a wealthy Bowerchalke family, was notorious in this connection, being one of the gentlemen hunters of the early eighteenth century who, attired in 'cap and jack', were quite happy to hunt in the vicinity of Vernditch and risk the £30 fine. Although fierce encounters between them and the keepers sometimes occurred, amicable relations seem to have been the general rule. Vernditch, with the area still known as the Chase, fringes the southern boundary of Bowerchalke, and Aubrey described it as having been a rich area for hunting, where buck, doe, fox and marten were seen in abundance.

A portrait of the notorious Harry Goode forms the frontispiece of Chafin's *History of the Chase* and the original can be seen in Dorchester Museum. His birth is the earliest entry of any kind to be found in the parish registers: 'April ye 8th Easter Day 1694, Henry Good son of Roger Good and Ann Good was born about eight of the clocke in the forenoone.' The family apparently continued to prosper for the burial register for 1789 states, 'Mrs Elanor Good, relict of Mr Henry Good, was brought from Wimborne Minster and buried *in linnen*, for which the poor of this parish received 50 shillings according to law. W. Coles Vicar.'

Care of the poor is mentioned in another connection at this time. In 1792, Poors Down, 10 acres of land situated on the western slopes of Marleycombe, was allotted in trust to the Lord of the Manor, the vicar and the churchwardens for the purpose of raising furze or other fuel for the use of all the poor parishioners and inhabitants of Bowerchalke. There was no restriction on the amount of furze which any individual could cut provided that it was carried away without having recourse to a cart or other vehicle. However, by Collett's time, it was rarely used for this purpose as very little furze remained. Eventually it was sold to a local farmer and the interest on the capital used by the trustees to provide a Christmas lunch for the elderly.

Edward Collett had a great passion for facts and figures and calculated that during the 600 years of his church's history – reckoned on an average of nine deaths per year – more than 5,000 people had been interred in the churchyard. It is sad that so little is known of these earlier inhabitants. Although parish records were made compulsory in 1530, those of Bowerchalke date only from 1701 (with the earlier birth of Harry Goode written as a memorandum on the flyleaf of the first burials register). They are contained in rather flimsy and tattered unbound books written on leaves of unruled parchment. The first baptism states baldly, 'MARY daughter of William Vaughan baptised April 6'; until 1813 no provision was made for other details such as the names of parents or the priest.

There are few instances of particular interest in the registers. In May 1763, Mr Henry White from Burcombe was buried, 'his death occasioned by being rode over', and on 11 September 1765, Hannah Herrington was killed by a waggon overturning and falling on her. Generally, however, it is the continuity of many Bowerchalke families that becomes apparent from a study of the early church records: the Hardimans were first mentioned in 1703, the Days in 1707 and the Foyles in 1709. The Pennys, Goldens, Targetts, Gullivers and Sheppards are among others still found up and down the valley today and in 1813 came the first mention of the Habgood family whose associations through farming, the Bell Inn, the Post Office and the church have continued to influence village life.

Historical reference to Bowerchalke in the early nineteenth century, apart from the parish registers, is scant although an edition of the *Salisbury and Winchester Journal* on 2 September 1822 gave an indication of the longevity of its inhabitants: 'There are now living in the small village of Bowerchalke 10 people whose united ages amount to 803, and 22 who are now more than 70.' In 1843, following the Tithe Commutation Act, a map was prepared by the Commissioners to assist their efforts in apportioning rent in lieu of tithes. By this time other new families including the Brachers and Coombs were established and the community was much as Collett found it on his arrival in 1878. The Census returns show very little variation in the population during the nineteenth century. This long-term social stability was common in country districts and is hardly surprising in south Wiltshire. There was little urban development to attract them elsewhere. Occasionally, younger sons would be drawn to the colonies or the army but generally the only significant movement was the Michaelmas Flitchings in October when farm labour was replaced or re-hired in preparation for the new cycle of agricultural activity.

A study of *Kelly's Directory* and the *Bowerchalke Almanacks* at the beginning of the 1880s show a largely self-sufficient community of 420 inhabitants with the new vicar established in his living, the gift of King's College, Cambridge, enjoying a modest income of £100 per annum and an ivy-covered vicarage of Chilmark stone. Wheat, barley and oats continued to be the main crops with sheep farming as a necessary adjunct, although dairy farming and the production of hay for animal feed played an increasingly important role. Josiah Williams, the Postmaster, lived in a cottage close to the vicarage, he was also the village carrier conveying passengers and orders to the Chough Inn, Salisbury every Tuesday,

James Foyle

Thursday and Saturday. Thomas Foyle, vicar's warden and captain of the bellringers, had developed his business of wheelwright, carpenter and undertaker with the help of his ten children, from a tiny cottage and yard opposite, while Edward Hardiman, leader of the Baptist community, ran the forge lower down Church Street. Here too, was the Bell Inn run by Isaac Habgood, baker, grocer, beer retailer, agent to the London and Provincial Fire Insurance Company and the Monarch Line of Steamers to America – a very busy man.

There were a surprising number of shops for so small a community. At the eastern end was a grocer and draper, Walter Welch, and further up the hill towards the church Mrs Sarah Bond, dressmaker, could be found. Between them, at the point where the yearly migration of frogs held up the traffic, John Lilley, shoemaker, lived in a diminutive one-roomed house which looked rather like a mushroom. At Sheppards Cross where religious and political open air meetings were frequently held, was William Penny's shop. His father, Charlie, had built the property in the 1850s as a squatter. At the western end where the road bends sharply into Woodminton were two maiden ladies, Martha and Henrietta Soffe providing groceries, confectionery such as treacle dumps and Sarum mints and material to make dresses. Known as West End Store, it was also licenced to sell vinegar, snuff and tobacco. Their only companion was Jeremiah, an eccentric old brother who would sit morosely outside their cottage shooting butterflies off his cabbages.

On the face of it, Bowerchalke would appear to have been a flourishing community, although the prosperity previously enjoyed by the farmers was steadily declining. Poor harvests and foreign competition had a disastrous effect on corn prices; between 1870–90, the acreage of wheat and barley throughout the chalkland region shrank by 25 per cent as more and more arable land was laid down to grass; further decline was caused by a sharp fall in the price of wool.

Agricultural labourers had never shared the earlier prosperity so for them conditions remained harsh. The weekly wage consisted of 10*s*. (50p) with 5*d*. deducted for cottage rent. This was for a day that started at 6 a.m. and finished at 5 p.m. six days a week. Even then, as Fred Penny recalls, pay was handed out on Saturday evenings and the younger workers would have to stand patiently by, sometimes for a long period, while the farmer discussed farming matters with his head carter, dairyman and shepherd. Gleaning, or leasing as it was known in Wiltshire, to eke out their meagre income was an annual activity, each cottage family gathering the loose grains from the harvested fields, traditionally sold in Bowerchalke to provide money for winter shoes. An amusing story related to me by Mrs Muriel Sheppard illustrates the extremes that poverty brought to them:

> *My uncle, George Bracher, used to live in my house. He told me of an old man who lived alone in one of the cottages next to the Baptist Chapel. Each week he took his washing to Mrs Stevens who lived in Quidham Street. This included his Sunday best shirt which without fail he collected every Saturday. One particular week he found he needed to wear his Sunday shirt for a very special occasion on the Friday. So off he went to collect it on the Thursday evening. He knocked on the door. No answer. Then a young boy leaned out of an upstairs window and shouted down – ' Thee cass'ent have un tonight, Father's got un on '.*

Low wages were supplemented by outdoor relief and when this was cut in 1883, Collett was not slow to express his disapproval:

> Several cases have lately occurred, in our parish, in which the Board of Guardians have reduced the allowance hitherto made to the poor, without – as it seems to us – sufficient reason. Unless some very good cause exists, it is hard that those in receipt of relief should be deprived even of a sixpence of that which they have been depending upon. We hope all those who have lately had their allowance reduced without real reason will protest against it.
>
> *Parish Papers* 4 August 1883

In 1886, there were fourteen persons on outdoor relief; by 1900 this had risen to thirty-one. For the aged and infirm there was always the workhouse

John Burton, ploughing the field opposite the Methodist Chapel, 27 August 1889

at Wilton and, in extremes, the County Asylum at Devizes. The incidence of mental instability in Wiltshire was high, not surprising perhaps, when one considers the appalling living conditions of many cottagers.

The decorative rose-covered cottages we see today are often an amalgam of several such dwellings and it is amazing how labourers, often with large families, could have existed cheek-by-jowl with their neighbours. 'Buddens', now a large single-family residence near the entrance to the village once housed three families, the diminutive 'Rose Cottage', (then known as 'Gaudy', or 'Gollicot Cottages'), housed another three. The Quidham Street cottages, clustered around Manor Farm, housed sixteen families then compared with the few that live there now, and at Woodminton, where Jasper Elliott and his son Charles farmed, ten families lived. At Chase, that strange community along the southern fringes of the downs, a scattered band of woodmen, shepherds, labourers and carters raised sufficient children to accommodate their own school.

Dampness, lack of ventilation, impure water and poor sanitation caused the illnesses which occurred with monotonous regularity. Collett was zealous in his belief that 'cleanliness was next to Godliness'. In 1883 an outbreak of cholera led him to urge the drinking of nothing but boiled water and two years later he advised:

> During this very hot weather, we strongly recommend, as a precautionary measure the prevalence of scrupulous cleanliness indoors and out and the

> burning, or burial, of all refuse; as well as the regular use of disinfectants, – such as Jeyes' Purifier, which may be bought at Mr Welch's at *3d.* a bottle. Fevers, cholera etc., to which we are so subject at this season, may often be thus prevented.

Consumption, bronchitis and influenza all took their toll while whooping cough, measles and chicken-pox decimated school attendance and sometimes closed the school for weeks at a time. One can sense the village sadness at the death of Lizzie Penny of influenza in 1892:

> The funeral of little Lizzie Penny which is to take place today at 3 will be one of exceptional interest and sadness. She was taken away after such a short sickness and has left behind her such pleasant memories of happy childhood that everyone mourns her loss. She will be followed to her grave by her fellow scholars in the Chapel Sunday School who will sing a hymn. . . .

In the winter of 1890 three babies died; in 1893 four of the schoolchildren died in as many months. Morrice Vincent, son of a village carrier at Misselfore was left completely deaf and dumb following an illness at the age of three. There were five other children in their tiny cottage and he was sent to a charitable home in London for severely handicapped children. Although vaccination is mentioned as early as 1887, smallpox was another

Mr and Mrs Butler of Rookery Farm, 1884

ever-present menace and following the outbreak of a particularly virulent strain in 1902 Collett again urged the importance of maintaining great cleanliness and the 'plentiful use of Lifebuoy soap', as well as the need to avoid contact with strangers in Salisbury.

The cottagers of Quidham Street were particularly prone to illness due to the impurity of the well water in that district, a matter Collett was quite prepared to take up with the landlord, Lord Pembroke:

> We think it is fully time that attention should be called to the lamentable condition of the water supply in Quidham Street. It is very scarce indeed, and very bad. Out of one of the wells we are told that insects are often drawn up on the surface of the water and occasionally such a thing as a dead frog makes its unwelcome appearance in the bucket. This state of things ought not to be possible and it is not surprising to find that Quidham Street is the unhealthiest part of the parish. We cannot imagine that so kind and considerate a landlord as the Earl of Pembroke is, would allow this dangerous state of things to continue if he did but know about it. We shall therefore forward him a copy of this paper and call his Lordship's personal attention to it.

A letter from Lord Pembroke later in the month acknowledged the problem and promised to see what could be done. No further reference is made to indicate whether or not his Lordship was as good as his word but two years later Collett was still complaining:

> Although the country air is healthier than that of the town there are a few things injurious: There is first the great deficiency of proper drainage leading to an accumulation of refuse which generates poisonous gases and often enough contaminates the water we drink by matter soaking into the earth and getting into the wells. Bad water is as fruitful a source of disease as bad smells. Then there is the danger arising out of the cottagers pig sty which very frequently is situated quite close to the house and poisons the otherwise pure air with its vile odours. And there are many other things equally obnoxious in producing disease.

All those cottagers who could afford it purchased a pig by paying quarterly subscriptions to the Pig Club secretary, Edward Hardiman Junior. At the Pig Club Meeting and Dinner in July 1883, for example, sixty persons were present and the 'bad smells' complained of by Collett would have been more than offset by the promise of things to come. Bought in the spring, the pig was kept in a small sty at the side of the house where it was fed on meal and vegetable scraps. There was a very competitive attitude towards the development of this prized possession, the sty being a focal point for neighbourly discussion. The Pig Club acted as a valuable safety net, for if the pig should die or fall ill the club reimbursed its members against losing their main source of winter meat. In the autumn the village

Mr Hermitage's cottage, May 1886

slaughterer, Frank Morns from Quidham Street, would have been very busy killing the animals (to the great distress of many doting children unable to ignore their squeals) and burning off the hair with wheat straw before cutting and salting the meat for the winter.

Accommodation for the farmer was, of course, considerably more commodious than that of the cottagers but was, nevertheless, quite spartan. Mrs Thelma Barter came to Woodminton Farm at the very end of Collett's ministry but there was still little comfort:

> *To begin with, I never liked the farmhouse. It was always dark, damp, and very cold in the winter. There was a range in the kitchen which worked well in bright weather, but when it was heavy and damp, it smoked and sulked and would not cook or throw out any heat.*
>
> *There was no water laid on; this had to be pumped up each day and we saved every drop. All the five children were bathed in the same water. The last one was very unlucky! After the bath, the water was used to wash the kitchen floor. The lighting was by oil lamps and candles. It was so cold that the pillow cases froze to the wall. Hot bricks were put in the beds to warm them for the children.*
>
> *The old scullery at the back, which is now Mrs Kennard's paved garden, was so cold that after the table had been washed, it froze. The snow drifted under the back door and came through the roof in places. There was an old-fashioned wood fire here round which lay sick and weakly lambs and calves. I have found twin calves lying on the mat in front of the range in the kitchen.*

All the children worked on the farm after school and in the holidays poor Richard led an old cart horse all day, during harvest when he was about six. They learned to deliver lambs at an early age. I also was made to do my share! Harvesting and haymaking were very hard work in those days. I also did an amount of veterinary work as I had been a nurse.

During the winter of 1882/3, soup at 1*d.* a pint had been provided at the vicarage door. As only three gallons at a time could be made applicants were restricted to a quart per family with the request that they brought their own jugs and cans. Originally coal was provided entirely through the generosity of Lord Pembroke, each cottager receiving 1½cwt. However, from 1887 he decided that a Coal Club should be created into which monthly payments could be paid by the labourers themselves during the six warmer months from April to September supplemented by a large subscription from him and the local tenant farmers, the coal being delivered by Edward Hardiman from the forge. A Clothing Club, under the energetic superintendence of Ellen Coombs, a farmer's wife, worked on a similar principle with goods bought at the end of the year from Henrietta Soffe's shop and John Dimmer (who had later taken over Walter Welch's business), at the other end of the village. Eventually, the two clubs were combined, the funds being supplemented by subscription from wealthier villagers and the profits of an occasional concert so that a bonus could be paid annually to each member according to how much he had subscribed. The system appears to have worked well, despite constant complaints that some people were unreliable in making their monthly payments, and it continued until the withdrawal of Lord Pembroke's support when he sold off his local estates in 1919.

Further encouragement of self-help was provided for women and children by a Medical Club – the Village Club protecting the men. Payment to the Medical Club was initially made to the Parish Clerk, William Wilkins, but when he died the local doctor received payment at his surgery in Broadchalke. In 1901, a more considerate practitioner, Dr Longman, arranged to collect them quarterly in the village schoolroom. A man in the village was paid 3*d.* to take messages to the surgery when help was needed and the doctor would arrive in his small four-wheeled carriage drawn by a single horse and driven by his groom-gardener. Hospital care, however, was more of a problem. Treatment at Salisbury Infirmary could only be obtained through the purchase of In-patient or Out-patient Orders. The Harvest Festival offertory was always used to obtain a supply of these for the poor and needy but there were rarely enough. This entry in the *Parish Paper* for 11 December 1902 has a typically desperate ring about it:

Infirmary letters have been in such great demand lately that out of the 12 we received at the end of last September we have *only three* left (one In-patient and

Miss Wood, Sunday school teacher and village benefactor, 23 August 1889

two Out-patient). We say this now to avoid disappointment to any who may count on getting admission to the Infirmary later on. When the remaining letters are gone we shall get no more until after next Harvest Festival.

Sometimes, as in this case, the shortfall was made up by generous readers of the *Parish Papers*, (probably Collett's intention) but there must have been many other occasions when assistance was not forthcoming.

The Liberal social reform legislation early this century undoubtedly helped to improve the lot of the poorer classes but much was still left to private initiative. In 1917 a trained nurse was appointed for the combined parishes of Broadchalke and Bowerchalke, each house contributing a small quarterly sum of 7½*d.* entitling them to the attendance of the nurse in times of sickness. Once more, this sum was supplemented by annual donations from local benefactors and the occasional concert or jumble sale. The first appointee, Nurse Smith, stayed but a few weeks and was replaced by Nurse Smithers from the Wiltshire Nursing Association. Fred Penny remembers her as a tall, thin lady cycling around the village in a brown uniform with fitting bonnet and lodging with Polly Foyle opposite the vicarage. His mother was one of the collectors of the Nursing Fund and a great friend of

The old post office blown down in a gale in 1897

Mr Welch's house and shop, 24 March 1886

hers. Collett speaks highly of her methods and the respect with which she was held.

Despite the prevalence of some illnesses, notably an epidemic of chicken-pox and whooping cough which closed the school for several weeks in 1921, the health of the village was responding to the general improvements in medical knowledge and the ministrations of the new nurse. An indication of this, perhaps, is the spate of bonny babies exhibited at baby shows which became popular from 1919, the first noted at a parish fête in Bishopstone when Bowerchalke infants carried off three of the prizes. A similar event in the village two years later attracted twelve prizes. Demonstrations of better methods of fruit and vegetable preparation at this time were also indicative of a more thoughtful approach to diet.

Communication through much of this period was ponderous and limited by the weather and poor road conditions. In 1881, for example, snow blocked the valley road for over a week and a storm in May the following year brought three large trees down across the road near the church obstructing all traffic for some time. The great storm of 1906 was remembered for years afterwards because of the damage to property and the killing of several cattle. Nevertheless, the weather did not deter some visitors who thought nothing of walking ten miles in order to preach or to take part in a village entertainment. Bicycles, too, became increasingly popular among those who could afford them.

It was the horse that remained the main motive power for agriculture, commerce and general movement of any distance despite the gradual encroachment of motor vehicles from the early nineteenth century. Josiah Williams was the main village carrier. In November 1881, he was also nominated by the villagers to be Postmaster when the office was established to replace the single wall-box that existed. His premises were a small mud-walled cottage with a smallholding and stabling adjacent to the vicarage. From here he ran both businesses until his death in 1888 when his daughter, Sarah Jane, took over the Post Office and his son Billie undertook the role of carrier, providing the main link with Salisbury. In his cumbersome waggon he conveyed passengers and luggage and brought orders back from the larger and more varied Salisbury shops. Collett quotes a fine description of the atmosphere of such a journey asserting with tongue-in-cheek that it could not possibly refer to his village as Bowerchalke had no gossips.

> For golden opportunities for gossip, what can surpass the Carriers cart? It goes so slowly to and from the market town; under its black hood the gossips are so snug and secure from interruption, from eaves dropping. The establishments of squire and parson, the doings of neighbour this and neighbour that, up street and down street – these are all overhauled in the Carriers cart. The ride to the market town in his vehicle is undoubtedly a treat – a distinct outing; and the shilling there and back is not high considering the

Gertrude Lloyd, the school monitoress, May 1886

> distance and the hills. In some cases the hills are so steep that the heavier folk get out and walk, and the horse is made to take a winding course and now and then there is a short rest when a stone is put behind the back wheels to ease the poor beast; but on the level the Carriers cart attains to a jog trot when the burden is light.

Apart from commerce, the carrier's covered brake was available to whoever wished to hire it. For example visits to gardens shows, fêtes and mission meetings in adjacent villages are mentioned. The rough roads could make the journey hazardous. On the way to Salisbury, while delivering goods, Billie Williams was once thrown from the van sustaining very bad bruising to his arm and shoulder. A more serious accident occurred in 1900 as he was travelling across the steep downs to Handley. His horse fell suddenly cutting both knees so badly that it had to be shot. Such a disaster to a carrier was, of course, catastrophic and it is much to the village's credit – as well as their own self-interest – that an ensuing collection raised sufficient money for him to purchase a new horse.

The Williams family ran their carrier service to the Chough Inn, Salisbury three times weekly. The journey was slow: Billie Williams would leave the village at 9.30 a.m. to arrive in Salisbury by 1 p.m. Stabling was provided at The Three Swans, (near what is now Macdonalds), and the cart would be left in procession with numerous others in Blue Boar Row. Fred Penny claims that although the waggon was always left unattended while Mr Williams went about his various commissions no parcel was ever stolen from it. The return journey commenced at 6 p.m., arriving home about 11 p.m. Billie Williams liked a drink and the slower journey home was due to his many pauses for refreshment at each of the valley taverns – often to the great annoyance of his passengers.

Billie Williams lived in one of the diminutive 'Gaudy Cottages' at the western end of the smallholding where he farmed and stabled his horse. Anna, his wife, a large genial woman, was one of a number of villagers who provided a holiday home for the parties of Greenwich children who came each summer. Monica Lee, who also spent her childhood holidays in the village with her father's family, the Habgoods, at the Bell, recalls Anna Williams as serving the dual role of midwife and layer-out.

> *When we saw her with a white apron and bag she was delivering a baby and when it was a black apron and bag she was laying out. We called her the bringer-in and the goer-outer!*

She had lost two children of her own: one at two years and the other stillborn.

A memorial tablet in the church is a sad reminder of another of the Williams' six children, Sidney, who died at the age of twenty. Sidney was a favourite of Collett's. A member of the choir from his youth, it was he who took the vicar to town in a small cart pulled by 'Coco', a brown pony. Later, as a private in the 10th Hussars, he served in South Africa before his posting to India where he contracted enteric fever at the Mhow Military Depôt in 1903. Two of his village friends and former choristers. Farrier Eddie Habgood and Corporal Alf Dimmer were with him when he died.

Another brother, Ernest, who lived with his family in an adjoining cottage, helped his father with his business. By 1915, however, the new motor service provided by the local farmer and watercress grower Robert Williamson had taken its toll on the carrier's trade. Now ailing, Billie Williams gave up the business and he died two years later, his son continuing to tend the smallholding and scratch a living from odd jobs.

The Post Office, taken over from Josiah by his daughter Sarah Jane Williams, suffered no such fate and developed steadily through the years. The sale of postal orders and a Sunday delivery of letters, fought so hard for by the Parish Council and Edward Collett through his Broadsheet were introduced in 1889. Three years later, Sarah Jane married Isaac Habgood Junior, son of the Bell Inn landlord. Known affectionately as 'Ikey', he was to remain as Postmaster at Bowerchalke until 1956 when he died aged eighty-eight, the oldest Postmaster in England. A great improvement to the postal service was effected in 1895 when a more efficient mailcart service between Salisbury and Tollard Royal brought quicker deliveries. Letters arrived at 5 a.m., and the delivery by 'Ikey' Habgood began at 7 a.m. In 1897 the old mud-walled premises collapsed in an overnight storm and new premises were opened at Sheppards Cross. Fred Penny remembers the mailcart as a very heavy horse-drawn box and when it arrived early in the morning the driver would tap on the Postmaster's upstairs window, 'Ikey' would then let down a rope with a hook at the end so the letters could be raised up in a sack for him to sort out in bed.

Collett described the travelling mailman, Charles Dowdern, as a 'beautiful example of strict punctuality, faithfulness and gentle conduct'. He, too, suffered from the perils of the roads and in 1895 was thrown violently from his seat, sustaining head injuries so bad that James Golden at Mead End had to take the mail to Tollard and bring it back in the evening. In 1912, as the van negotiated the treacherous Chase Hill, the horse took fright at the sound of the brake just before the sharp turn into Woodminton and bolted down the steep incline. The driver was again thrown violently from the van and picked-up in a semi-conscious condition. Having lost a lot of blood he

Mr Burrough's house, Bowerchalke, 1885

was carried into a cottage for attention. The horse had meanwhile careered into a hedge and lay stunned in the adjoining orchard. Neither it nor the van were badly damaged and after a couple of hours the journey was able to be resumed. A few years later a third similar accident was recorded on the Broadchalke road.

In 1899 money orders could be purchased, but not cashed, and a Savings Bank was established in the Post Office. Attempts to get a second delivery of letters, despite many exhortations, were not successful until 1913 and the nearest telegraph office remained at Broadchalke. Sarah Jane's death and the introduction of the first Post Office motor van came in 1915, and at the same time as her brother William had given up his carrying business. The long influence of the family on village life, over four generations, was almost at an end.

No disaster affected Bowerchalke during this period to compare with the terrible calamity across the downs at Sixpenny Handley in May 1892 when fire destroyed nearly all the main street including over sixty homes. This is particularly surprising considering that most of the Bowerchalke houses were thatched and people lived so close together using the most rudimentary methods of cooking. The fire at Charles Elliott's Woodminton farm in August 1901, however, illustrates the difficulties of providing effective aid once a fire occurred. Charles Elliott, chairman of the Parish Council, churchwarden and one of Bowerchalke's busiest citizens, was just on the point of following the rest of his family to matins when clouds of smoke were seen issuing from his valuable hayrick. Many neighbours were quickly on the spot to provide assistance but the nearest fire engine, eight miles away at Wilton Park, was not able to arrive until over an hour later and even that was at a speed that Collett – while grumbling about the effect the excitement had had on his church service – regarded as commendable.

Not surprisingly, most accidents were connected with work and usually concerned livestock. Carter Munday, for example, in 1883 on his way back from Salisbury was thrown from his waggon, trampled on and run over by the wheel. He was treated at Broadchalke by the local doctor and then conveyed to Salisbury Infirmary in an empty coal cart that happened to be passing. Similar accidents are recorded as happening to both Samuel Pitman, thrown from his milk van, and Tom Randell, from his coal waggon, as well as the numerous accidents to the postman. Joseph Golden, a woodsman working on the Chase, was killed in 1907 when he fell from the tailboard of his donkey cart. On the farm things could be just as hazardous. Incidents such as that recorded in the same year when a dairyman was badly crushed trying to control a rebellious cow, are fairly common and on Butler's Farm at Rookhaye in 1910 two labourers fell 16 ft from a ladder when working on a rick.

The Williamson's prize bull, 1889

Accidents to pedestrians in this more leisurely age were practically non-existent but the increasingly popular pastime of cycling must have caused a few bruises especially before efficient brakes and tyres were developed. Fred Penny, despite having his foot amputated as a child, thought nothing of cycling to his brother's home at Hayling Island and his father, William, was the first person in the village to own one of the more contemporary-styled 'safety bicycles', replacing his penny farthing. For the farm labourer in 1904 a good secondhand model could be purchased from Mr Lloyd at the Canal, Salisbury for £3; a price which made it a practical proposition. Mr Penfound, the schoolmaster, was 'thrown' from his bicycle, (a term still redolent of horses), in 1913 on his way back from a County Council lecture at Ebbesbourne Wake, sustaining nasty cuts and bruises and the new school attendance officer was off work for some time following a similar experience.

In the same year, 1916, Mr Penfound's sister, Kate, became the first recorded road fatality caused by a motor vehicle when she was killed in Salisbury. By now such vehicles had thrown off their self-conscious, innovatory image and the crash in 1917 when Henry Butler and a friend were badly injured running up a bank was probably due as much to zealous over-confidence than to anything else. For most people cycling still remained the only self-owned form of transport they could afford. On the relatively safe roads there was little to worry the unwary and when Harry Taylor was killed in 1920 whilst venturing out onto the busier Bournemouth roads he was eighty-five years old.

News of its sons further afield drifted back to the village through letters or, occasionally, the press. A 21 year-old, Henry Greenstock, was killed while on duty on the railway at Eastleigh in 1899. Over twenty of his fellow porters made the journey to Bowerchalke for the service and contributed generously to the funeral expenses. Links with the sea were tenuous for this land-locked community, although William Harding from Manor Farm had the misfortune to be shipwrecked in 1913. On a short sea voyage for the benefit of his health in the royal steamship *Agadir* the vessel hit a reef off the coast of Morocco. Fortunately, it did not founder and all the passengers were eventually saved.

More tragic was the death of Tom Kerley a chef on the ill-fated *Titanic*. His parents who worked on the Elliott's farm were very proud of their smart and popular son and especially of his progress to the largest and most magnificent ship of its day. Kate Gulliver, who lived on the Chase remembers the terrible gloom that sinking cast over the whole country. At a memorial service for Tom in the Baptist Chapel his father asked for the boy's favourite hymn, 'Peace Perfect Peace' and wept throughout the singing of it.

Tom Kerley's death was noted in the 24 April 1912 edition of the *Parish Paper* but a strange sequel was noted later:

> A sad sequel to the tragic drowning of young Tom Kerley in the ill-fated *Titanic* has come by the news of the unexpected recovery of his lifeless body floating in mid-ocean. It was noticed by a passing vessel homeward bound. With reverent care it was up lifted and after the Burial Service had been said once more committed to the deep to the grand and solemn music of the ever restless waves.

Most travellers would not have enjoyed the same standard of luxury as those unfortunate passengers on the *Titanic*. Throughout the period young men from many local families, hungry for employment and adventure, joined the steady flow to the colonies, especially to Canada and Australia. Sometimes, when there was a particularly necessitous case, the village would help defray the expenses. Polly Coombs, a housemaid in Sherborne, suffered from fainting fits and although her employer spoke highly of her ability, because of her condition, he felt unable to allow her to continue. Her brother William in Australia offered her a home and the villagers helped to raise the £6 needed for her passage. The journey took several weeks during which there were three burials at sea. She suffered greatly from

Lizzie Habgood, 28 July 1889

sickness and the extreme heat and must have been very relieved to reach Sydney where her brother was waiting for her with his wife and eight boys.

Legends of the past were embedded deep in the village psyche and were told and re-told to generations of children so that Bowerchalke came to be referred to as the most haunted village in Wiltshire. Because of their lack of authenticity many of these accounts have been related separately in the Appendix to this work, but the strongest and most plausible story is that of Kit, an old gypsy woman, who committed suicide by throwing herself in a well now hidden beneath a car park at the side of the vicarage. As suicides were not buried in consecrated ground her body was taken to the boundary mark of Wiltshire, Dorset and Hampshire in Vernditch, where the outline of her alleged grave will still be shown to you. Collett was very good to the gypsies who frequently congregated near the village, so much so that his kindly nature was rather taken advantage of. His habit of giving a shilling to a new baby became so well known that several different families would present the same baby if he was not careful. John Linnell, who took care of all the vicar's domestic arrangements, tried to guard against his gullibility but Collett retained his fondness for them despite their devious ways:

> Gipsies seem to have been very plentiful in our neighbourhood lately but they are now always welcomed when they give us a call. It seems difficult to understand their tramping manner of life and they are generally treated with suspicion although there may be a number of worthy folk among them.

Other familiar itinerants passing through the dusty country roads were a common sight, far commoner than today. One such poor creature was mentioned in 1913:

> ANGELINA, A TRAMP – A well-known figure has passed into the unseen world. After her sad wanderings in a pitiless world the end came suddenly by drowning. May God have mercy on her soul.

Another was Joseph Cook, a cheapjack, who visited the village regularly with his wares. Like so many others mentioned, he was thrown from his van on the rough roads and taken unconscious to the Infirmary where he died the following day.

Death, disaster, sickness and disease; life at that time must have seemed a very chancy affair. The Village Club, or Bowerchalke Union Friendly Society to give it its full name, was the only protection that most of the villagers could hope for against the worst effects of misfortune. Started in 1864 it provided, through the annual subscriptions of its members, an avenue of support when doctors' fees or funeral expenses had to be paid and a bond of fellowship in an area of activity where trade union organisation was particularly weak. The importance of this collective form of self-help is illustrated by the death of James Harte, a farm labourer, in 1903. He had been receiving medical treatment for a considerable time, being an out-patient of the Infirmary. Although he was aware of his critical condition necessity compelled him to work when he could and following a heavy day's threshing he died in his sleep. The consternation felt by the villagers at losing a popular member of their community was heightened by the fact that his widow and children were left practically penniless 'on account of his not having been able to keep up his Club Membership.'

The importance of the Village Club can be further illustrated when in 1892 it ran into financial difficulties. Members agreed to help by paying an extra annual fee for medical attention so as to relieve working expenses which would have been sufficient had a bad influenza epidemic in the early months not made heavy and continuous demands on the sick pay fund. Further entreaties were made for new members in order to boost their capital and for every member with money on his private account to transfer it to the General Sick Fund. It says something for the common bond that fifty-four members were ready to do this and only seven refused.

As a contrast to the bleaker aspects of the club activities it provided its members and their families with perhaps its most memorable annual event, the Whitsun Feast Day. When Collett first arrived it was the custom to hold the event over two days with drunkenness and high spirits getting out of hand. In 1885, he wrote: 'We are sorry to hear that the Club Feast is this year to be continued over the Thursday as well as the Wednesday. It is much to be hoped that the Club Committee will use their influence to prevent this happening again both on the score of economy to the Club funds and in the moral interests of the people.' Despite this plea it continued over two days until the aforementioned financial difficulties when wiser heads prevailed. Certainly from that time standards of behaviour did improve.

Descriptions of the Club Feast in the *Parish Papers* and *Salisbury Times* indicate that the procedure varied very little. The members would meet on the lawn of John Coombs' farmhouse, complete with their colourful banner and sashes and collars of rich red silk for the main officials. Led by the local brass band they walked to the church for an 11 o'clock service where the sermon was always given by a visiting minister. The procession would then continue its perambulation of the village finishing up at Binghams Farm where Robert Williamson's barn provided the venue for the feast. Accounts show a wide selection of mutton, roast beef, ham, vegetables, salad and

Josiah Williamson, village carrier, outside the vicarage in 1884

beer for this grand occasion. In the ensuing speeches honorary members of the Club, including many of the local farmers, and other guests were welcomed, the health of the King proposed, songs sung, and a report given by the secretary on the up-to-date position of the Society's funds which seem to have prospered quite well after its low point in 1892.

The children were not forgotten on these occasions. Isaac Sheppard, mentioned previously as one of the village's most generous and successful benefactors, always liked to return to his home village for the Club Day and he presented the children with a bun and an orange. Greta Case remembers the Club Day as the highlight of her year:

> *My grandfather James Penny, who was head shepherd for Mr Williamson, carried the flag for years. He was very proud of this and got excited for days beforehand. We marched up the street to the Church and then on to Woodminton, back up Quidham Street and round the back lane to Binghams Yard for a dinner. The women used to be cooking and roasting the beef and on Thursday night there would be a supper with the leftovers. Some people called Haines came with the old-fashioned swingboats, roundabouts, a shooting gallery and other stalls. These were erected in a gaily-decorated field opposite to Binghams where Mr Coombs kept his cows. It was all very exciting.*

The Club Day in 1911 was dwarfed by more important preparations; the Coronation of King George V was to be celebrated throughout the land and Bowerchalke was not to be left out. A committee of village dignatories met well in advance to plan the events and on a warm June day everything passed off successfully. A short church service included the singing of a special coronation version of the National Anthem and was followed by a dinner, this time at Rookhaye, for all those over fourteen who had paid their shilling. The children enjoyed a very fine tea and the evening was given over to games, including tug-of-war between farm teams as well as races for children, women and even the pensioners. The village band played and dancing in the gathering dusk brought the day to a satisfactory conclusion.

Many such occasions to celebrate national events marked the years: Victoria's Jubilee, royal marriages, the celebration of peace after the First World War all brought a little colour into the normal round of village life. The Club Day, however, remains focussed in people's minds as the event of their summer. In 1911, with the passing of the National Insurance Act, the reason for its existence was threatened. In 1912 the event passed off joyously enough, marked by the attendance of Walter Butler after twenty-five years absence in Australia, but a few days later came the official notice that all workers were to be insured through the national scheme. Edward Collett, with a countryman's innate suspicion of innovation remarked, 'We always imagined that England was a free country! But it does not look like it nowadays.' In the following year, although the sun shone, the band played attractively and the speeches were as hearty as ever, the numbers had dwindled.

In 1914, with the clouds of war gathering, Collett bemoaned the declining vitality of village life:

> It seems to be more or less uncertain as to whether the whitsuntide fête shall be held this year or not. For so very many years past it has been the principal holiday of the early summer as well as a time of reunion between friends and neighbours that we sincerely hope it may if possible not be allowed to drop out of existence.

The Club staggered on for a further year but in March 1915 it was officially discontinued, a meeting being held in the schoolroom to pay out its funds. Although the villagers were to benefit from the security of properly established welfare provisions, an institution which had lasted over fifty years was brought to an end.

4
The Church

A church on the present site at Bowerchalke was mentioned as early as 1298, but probably existed much earlier than that. It originally consisted of nave, chancel and transepts forming the usual cruciform pattern. In 1866 the church, like so many others in Victorian times, underwent heavy restoration by a Mr T.H. Wyatt of London. In his *Bowerchalke Almanack* of 1883, Collett stated that a south aisle was constructed and this explains the rather unusual profile of the church from the north-west. A new pulpit was added, alterations were made to the font and Bishop Hamilton generously donated a larger altar table, which still dominates the east end. The new altar windows above it were given by Lady Herbert of Lea, the mother of the Earl of Pembroke. At the west end the gallery was taken down, although the entrance to it can still be seen from the belfry. In the nave, the high box pews were replaced by the rather bland fixtures that we see today. The tower was raised some 10 ft, a feature that stands out prominently on Collett's photographs of 1884, and provided with new battlements and gargoyles.

The work was completed at a cost of £1,500, a sum borrowed from the Commissioners of Public Works which was repayable over the next twenty years on the security of the rates and the church officially re-opened at a special service on Thursday 15 March 1866. The vicar at that time was Dr Rowland Williams, a distinguished scholar who had previously been a fellow of King's College, Cambridge and Vice Principal of St David's College, Lampeter. He must have worked very hard overseeing the alterations especially as he lived in the main parish of Broadchalke two miles away. Following the re-opening he wrote to his sister: 'Yesterday went off well in spite of a heavy downpour. The Bishop of Ely preached beautifully. The church looks almost perfect in its kind having as much of the quietly ornamental as a rural district desires.'

This newly-renovated structure was what Edward Collett would have inherited a few years later in 1878 but, as stated earlier, with a somewhat

Bowerchalke Church in 1884 – the extension to the tower can be clearly seen

apathetic church community. Returns to a questionnaire sent by the Bishop of Salisbury to all parishes in 1783 indicate that there was little church activity at that period. There was a single service at 1 p.m., a strange time to have it but the curate, who lived at Broadchalke, had three churches to preside over. They were some distance apart and travel would have been slow. The Revd W. Taprell Allen, for example, writing to Collett in April 1887 said: 'When at Bowerchalke I had also charge of Alvediston and often when riding over the downs, along a mere sheep walk I have found myself completely enveloped in a sea fog and obliged to trust to my pony.' At what stage a curate took up residence in Bowerchalke is not clear but the services, as an indicator of church activity, seem to have increased very little. Collett tells us that on his arrival evensong was held at 3 p.m. and Holy Communion monthly at midday; there is no mention of a morning service.

The Nonconformists, on the other hand, were undoubtedly strong at this time. Out of a population of 420, most of whom were of the labouring class, a great proportion of the farmers and people were Dissenters. The Methodist Chapel was completed a year after Collett arrived and the Baptist Chapel, built in 1858, was replaced in 1897 by a new one built alongside.

Mrs Wood, 20 September 1888. There is a window in the church in her memory

The older chapel was converted to a Sunday school and, from 1902, this became a Reading Room for young men in the village. When Collett arrived the Baptists had just completed a highly successful period of thirteen years under the charismatic leadership of their pastor John Hockey. The vicar refered scornfully to their services as 'Parliamentary' affairs, having a human rather than divine foundation, while Collett is referred to, even amongst his own party, as 'an extreme ritualist'. It is not surprising, therefore, that in religious terms they found it difficult at times to get along and the lines were drawn for a battle of words that erupted on occasions throughout the years in the *Parish Papers* and elsewhere. In 1906, for example, Collett wrote: 'According to a paragraph in the *Daily Express* there is a parish in Essex, High Roothing, with a population of 400 in which there is not a single dissenter. It seems to be much too good to be true but we sincerely hope it is, for to think of a parish without schism is as sweet as a glimpse of Heaven.' However, this was withdrawn before going to press.

Despite these problems Collett was determined to build up his church community as the central focus of village life. The *Bowerchalke Almanack*, published by him in the vicarage and given free each year to church members and other interested parties, shows that by 1883 there was, for the first time, a flourishing choir of senior and junior choristers. His notes and photographs throughout the '80s indicate a church awash with colour, the altar emblazoned by numerous candles and with services to celebrate every conceivable occasion. If his style seemed somewhat theatrical the villagers must, nevertheless, have been impressed by his industry. By Easter 1882 he had established sufficient confidence to say in his *Paper*, 'It is *particularly* requested that the Communicants will all make a *special* effort to attend the FOUR O'CLOCK CELEBRATION in preference to any other' (Collett had underlined those words italicised). Other services, however, followed at regular intervals throughout the day.

The *Parish Papers* record fully the annual round of the church calendar often supplemented by services of Collett's own invention. There are valuable insights, for example, into the Victorian inclination towards elaborate funerals although, perhaps surprisingly, he did not seem to favour overdressing for the occasion wanting 'no gloomy-looking hat bands or other such unChristianlike monstrosity disfiguring the solemnity.' In 1881, at the funeral of the seamstress Emma Jane Bond, he introduced for the first time a full choral service with a violet pall to cover the coffin. In 1885 he laid down more fully his expectations for such occasions, 'Usefulness and hideous so-called "ornaments" of heathenish looking urns and weeping cherubs on the coffin, are to be avoided, punctuality is essential and post-funeral feasts should not be indulged in.'

The funeral of Mrs Ann Williams, the Postmaster's wife, in 1886 gives a particularly interesting picture of the formality of the occasion:

> The funeral of Mrs Williams was chorally rendered, the greater part of the Choir being present. At 3 o'clock the surpliced procession – headed by the Cross bearer – went up to the house of mourning, waiting at the gate until the BODY was brought out, covered with the Violet Pall, on which rested the wreaths, and crosses, of white Azaleas, and other flowers, speaking of the endless bloom wherewith the Saints at rest are crowned. On the way back to Church, the Hymn 'Thy Will Be Done' was sung. Both of the Proper Psalms were chanted, and after the Lesson, 'Now the labourer's task is o'er' was sung, before the BODY of her who had so often worshipped in that Church was taken out for the last time.
>
> As all the chief mourners had been at the early Celebration on the day of the funeral, trying there to learn how to confide their sorrows in the Love and Sympathy of an ever present Saviour, and to beseech His mercy on the departed, it was with deep meaning that we sang 'O Paradise' on our way to the grave, telling of our faith that 'Loyal hearts and true, stand ever in the Light'. When the BODY was being lowered into the ground, we had Hymn 401, and after the service was done, the choir returned to the Church. . . . Muffled Peals were rung on the Bells after the Burial Service was over.
>
> *Parish Paper* 22 January 1886

This provides a sad contrast to the procedure to be adopted for suicides or, as in this case, an unbaptized child in the previous year:

> The death of an unbaptized child (daughter of Mr Joseph Witt), has occurred during this week. The little girl was at school on Tuesday 14th and died, – from malignant sore throat, and croop – on Sunday morning last aged 9. As the church service cannot be used for her, her death will give rise to the first lay burial in this parish, under the recent Act of Parliament. The body will of course not be taken into the church, nor will the Dead Bell be tolled.
>
> *Parish Papers* 24 July 1885

Today, although Harvest Festival still remains a popular service, it has far less of the immediacy of earlier years when food was grown and consumed locally. In 1902, for example, Collett wrote:

> There can be no question at all about the serious nature of the rough weather we have had, so far as the harvest is concerned. It is much to be regretted and the sight of the dripping sheaves waiting to be garnered and of the anxious labourers standing idle and helpless is a saddening one.
>
> *Parish Papers* 4 September 1902

The Harvest Festival service, which Collett introduced in October 1879 with its sixty altar candles and coloured stoles, may have caused two people to walk out in protest but continual reports in the local newspapers, as well as his own paper, indicate its popularity with the majority of villagers, stamped as it was with the vicar's usual flair. Unlike today, when only one service takes place, Collett underlined the importance of the occasion with a full 'octave', consisting of a full day of services on two successive Sundays. The climax was evensong on the first Sabbath when a solemn procession of young choristers bearing richly-laden baskets of corn, fruit and flowers would follow the processional cross to the steps of the altar where the vicar would be waiting to receive the offerings. The church was richly decorated in every nook and cranny by the ladies of the village, with rows of white flowers encircling the font and clusters of rosy and golden apples embedded in moss. Profusions of double and single dahlias in different colours lined the chancel interspersed with double sunflowers in pots. Strangely, no vegetables were ever displayed although arrangements were made for them to be collected by Mrs Coombs, the churchwarden's wife, and taken to Salisbury Infirmary.

Even more spectacular was a service Collett introduced in 1884 which appears to have been unique to Bowerchalke – the Hay Harvest Festival. Collett's arrival in the village coincided with a severe depression in farming which lasted until 1914. It was marked by rapidly declining prices for farm produce, especially corn, as cheap imports flooded in from the United

States and Canada, causing great hardship for the farmers, many of whom went out of business or were forced to radically alter the whole pattern of their farming. The situation was made worse by a succession of cold, wet springs and summers followed by disastrously poor harvests. In August 1888 Collett observed:

> There can be but one opinion as to the increasingly serious aspect of matters owing to the extraordinary quantity of rain with which we are being visited this season together with the absence of sunshine. The hay crops were materially affected and now it seems possible that the more important corn harvest may suffer as well.

This hit the downland farmers particularly badly as they were dependent on corn growing for the greater part of their livelihood. The decline in corn growing also affected the sheep. The wet seasons had already reduced their numbers due to footrot, but the decline in corn acreage caused whole flocks to disappear, their prime purpose having been, not wool as most people imagine, but the maintenance of fertile arable land by folding, a process whereby the flock would be enclosed nightly in different portions of the fields.

As farmers found it more profitable to sow their land with grass rather than wheat, the process of haymaking became increasingly more important, providing a plentiful supply of food for farm animals. The Hay Harvest Festival, which evolved in Bowerchalke from this background, took place on the second Sunday in July when the hay had been 'well won', to use the terminology of farmers of the time, although occasionally it had to be postponed if the weather caused delays. Preparations seem to have started well in advance for the decorations were by no means confined to hay. It was, in Collett's words, 'a bright service to commemorate the ingathering of the hay and to thank God for the flowers of the field.' The children, even those as young as three or four, could be seen after school dotted about the fields and lanes gathering grasses and wild flowers. Gardens would be scoured for their choicest blooms. These would be brought back to the church where, in the days before the festival, they would ripen in the sunshine before being worked into wreaths and intricate patterns by skilled hands.

The first celebration of the Hay Harvest, held in 1884, was widely reported in the local press and was to set the pattern for all future events. The altar, surmounted by large banners, was decked with its festive white frontal and illuminated with a profusion of candles. A temporary screen was erected at the entrance to the chancel which was covered with grasses and wild flowers. The font was colourfully decorated with floral displays, grasses, delicate ferns and surmounted by a pair of vases brimming with flowers, the pulpit with grasses interwoven with poppies and big ox-eye daisies. Flower pots lined the chancel aisle, the highly-scented lily adding a richness to the atmosphere.

Services took place throughout the day culminating at 6.15 p.m. when the ringers met to peal the bells for evensong. Then the crucifer, holding high the processional cross, elaborately covered with grasses and white roses, led the younger choristers through the nave to lay bouquets of wild flowers and sheaves of ornamental grasses onto the altar. Father Collett, as he was often known, or his special preacher of the day would address the congregation in terms suitable for the occasion and the service would end with a solemn rendering of the Te Deum.

As the popularity of the Hay Harvest Festival increased, the congregation was swollen by people who made the journey, often over long distances on foot, from other parishes and the festivities extended to a full 'octave' of two whole Sundays. An evening service with a guest preacher was held midweek. The children, too, had a special midweek service to which they brought posies of tightly-bound flowers. These were later placed on graves in the churchyard or sent to the Children's Ward in Salisbury Infirmary. Old friends were invited to send their contributions to the Hay Harvest from afar and grasses are mentioned as arriving from as far off as Kent, Devon, Nottingham and Guernsey, 'to represent the bonds of spiritual and brotherly unity between us in our common unity.'

A happy picture of the Sunday school outing to Bournemouth, July 1921

In 1885, following the death of George Moberly, Bishop of Salisbury, tokens of mourning were placed in the church during the Hay Harvest and the processional cross veiled with black crêpe. However, two years later, a far happier occasion took place for the festivities included the first confirmation service in Bowerchalke within living memory. It was taken by the new Bishop, John Wordsworth, a man for whom Collett had a great admiration, and it was his first official visit to the parish. To mark the occasion all the church members sat down at 4 p.m. to an excellent tea to await his arrival. The village had been gaily decorated, flags were hung out and over the school gate, opposite the church, an archway of evergreens, was placed made entirely by the children and surmounted by the words, 'The Children's Welcome'. Another archway was erected at the church gate and a third at the vicarage. At the entrance to the village, further decorated with the word 'Welcome', the Bowerchalke Brass Band greeted the Bishop and preceded him to the vicarage, where the church bells rang merrily as he approached. The Bishop and a lady friend were riding on horseback, with Mrs Wordsworth and another lady accompanying him in an open carriage. After a short rest the Bishop and his party joined the communicants at tea in the school during which the band played selections in the schoolyard. Before the service began Edward Collett presented the Bishop with a framed picture of the church and made an address of welcome from the communicants to mark the occasion.

Flowers in abundance adorned the church throughout its yearly calendar and the 'kindly neighbour' act of sending flowers from afar was not restricted to the Hay Harvest. Ascension Day was made resplendent by the diminutive forget-me-not, suggestive as Collett said, 'of the loving remembrance that Christians have of their ascended Lord.' Strange that such insignificant little blooms should assume such importance that they were sent long distances:

> GIFTS – with her usual great kindness Miss Freeth has sent us Altar flowers (from Jersey) for the Ascension Festival. Rev Poulton also forwarded flowers from Devonshire with the friendly wish that they might 'find a place in dear old Bowerchalke'. And from Essex came the gift of a large box of forget me nots sent by Bessie Golden.
>
> *Parish Papers* 20 May 1909

For the Easter octave, the church was decorated with masses of wild primroses in juxtaposition with exotic hothouse flowers and various pot plants. Even at Christmas the church was adorned with beautiful white chrysanthemums. One occasion not celebrated with flowers, however, was 'Fragment Sunday', Collett's name for the sad drop in attendance that usually follows every great festival, when the devil – 'he doesn't deserve a capital letter!' – is able to gather up the remnants!

Despite his ritualistic style and high moral purpose, there was little pompousness about Father Collett; he was able to see and appreciate humour on many occasions when others might have expressed annoyance:

> Just at the beginning of the Creed while the accompanying chords were being played there was a sudden bang followed by a frantic effort, at express speed, on the part of our little friend the 'puffer' (Teddy Davis) to keep up the wind! It was found necessary to do without the harmonium for the rest of the service. The disaster was afterwards easily remedied as it was only one of the bellows strings that had given way. So at evensong the organist was again serenely exercising her powers and the puffer calmly supplying the wind, as though there were no such thing in the world as 'organ-ic' disease!
>
> *Parish Papers* 5 October 1899

Mrs Christine Gulliver, previously landlady of the Bell Inn, also relates a story her father, Edward Habgood, told her about Collett's ability to see the funny side of things. He always gave details of the last hymn from the pulpit. On one occasion he meant to announce one starting, 'Conquering Kings their titles take', but accidentally said, 'kinkering conks' and broke out into loud peals of laughter.

A group of confirmation candidates, July 1889

Mission services were also very popular, an annual event often linked with a magic lantern lecture in the schoolroom. They were usually sponsored by the Society for the Propagation of the Gospel (SPG), which the church supported. On such occasions speakers brought to this tiny country village a vision of mysterious places like Honolulu and Madagascar whose primitive peoples and customs must have seemed as incomprehensible as if they had come from the moon. The fascination was even more pronounced when, as in 1901, the visit was accompanied by an exhibition. An elephant god, a shield made of human skulls, poisoned arrows, a model of a Chinese lady's foot were just a few of the curios displayed at that time.

The church porch, a gathering-place for the faithful, contained a rather special letterbox. Collett would never have seen himself as a precursor of the modern 'agony aunt', but in ecclesiastical terms he provided quite a valuable service to the timid and insecure seeker after truth. By means of this porch box people could ask, anonymously, questions about doctrine and their faith, a reply being given in the form of a sermon in the following week's evensong or in the *Parish Paper*. It was, of course, open to abuse. In 1885, for example, a Dissenter used it provocatively to raise once more the thorny question of church baptism debated so heatedly at the village conference three years earlier. Collett did not flinch from replying in equally bigoted terms:

> . . . To an honest enquirer seeking instruction in the faith, (for its own sake, and not for the purpose of strife), we would most gladly have given a reply to the best of our power. But we do not consider it either necessary or expedient to use our very limited space in answering the captious letters of such persons as our present anonymous correspondent, to whom we would suggest that a man who has never even learnt to spell, is hardly in a position to set his learning before the world, or to expect to overrule the doctrine of the Christian church.
>
> *Parish Papers* 24 April 1885

The church porch was also the gathering-place for another group of faithful. Each May the returning swallows would swoop around the tower and make their nests in the belfry and bell chamber. Their presence, symbolic of approaching summer, was always welcome but Collett fought a constant battle to keep them out of the porch. For years he reminded parishioners to keep the outer door shut while the swallows were building their nests. In 1910, quite mysteriously, they seem to have taken the hint. One correspondent suggests that it was because of declining numbers, many being killed for the adornment of ladies' hats. That being the case, Collett retorted, the *total* extinction of the swallow would have already been accomplished considering 'the very enormous and ugly umbrella-sized hats which women put on their heads just now!'

The First World War brought services of a more solemn nature but, also, touches of humour. The insistence in February 1916 that all lights in houses and churches should be veiled an hour and a half before sunset caused some annoyance. The nave windows were shaded with a coat of green paint and the transept windows curtained making it necessary to bring the evening service forward half-an-hour. The new Daylight Saving Act in May of that year by which clocks were to be put forward one hour caused even more bewilderment in a community where the daily round of sunrise and sunset ruled everyone's lives. Collett conceded that the railway and the Post Office would need to follow the new time but was at a loss to know whether others would follow suit. For the time being, therefore, he decided that the church services should be at their customary time until things sorted themselves out, even though 'the hands of the clock will point to the imaginary and fanciful Government time!'

An even more amusing crisis arose at the Methodist Chapel, the preacher for the morning service, Mr Gifford of Compton Abbas failed to arrive and, in his absence, Mrs Charles Butler led the worship. However, at 11.55 a.m., Mr Gifford walked in, astonished to find the service nearly over. On being reminded that the nation had put its clocks forward the previous night, he replied innocently, 'I never thought you'd take any notice of that, friends!'

Although Collett was gratified by the gradually increasing size of his church community, he was not slow to point out from the pulpit and in his *Parish Papers* the human frailties of his congregation. Knowing what a strange fascination lurked in the sound of the late opening of the door he constantly berated late arrivals. Talking aloud before the service began while warming their toes at the grating or in the church porch afterwards was considered to be disrespectful to the majesty of God. The 'selfish and ugly' habit of propping themselves up on two hassocks instead of one to the deprivation of others was a sign of laziness. There are constant reprimands to the younger members of the congregation whose irreverent behaviour, especially behind the font, he warns, could render them, according to the law of the land, to a fine not exceeding £5 or two months' imprisonment. Rather excessive, perhaps, by modern standards but his tirade against the theft of a penny hymn book from the porch was obviously effective as prompt restitution by the guilty party was made the following week. Neither did he care for the meanness of those who took advantage of the secrecy of the offertory bag to give smaller coins than he expected: 'there is a coppery sound about the matter which brings little credit to any of us and which we hope will assume a more silvery note before another year!'

Nor was Collett himself free of criticism, (although he did not report these in the *Parish Papers*, preferring to keep such reports to the privacy of his scrapbooks). In April 1881, for example, he was invited to present a

Bowerchalke church decorated for the Hay harvest service, 1885. Edward Collett introduced this particular festival to the parish

paper at the Church of England Sunday School Institution held at St Edmunds Schoolroom, Salisbury, during the course of which he maintained that the Bible was too difficult a book to be placed in the hands of children and that a 'free Bible' would not mean its better use. For these views he was branded in the local press by indignant readers as an extreme ritualist hawking Romish ideas. Ten years later the *Western Gazette* took him to task for not allowing the choir to attend a parishioner's funeral because the choir surplices were being washed in preparation for Easter. The *Swindon Advertiser* of 9 May 1891 took this up, devoting four columns to a scathing and satirical attack on him for his extremism.

The churchyard was a constant source of concern to him. The mischievous antics of children who scampered amongst the graves and picked the snowdrops were a trial, as in his view were the adults who seem to have been equally misguided. Sham flowers under glass covers placed on the graves instead of fresh flowers were an abomination to him but pickle bottles and jam jars, still labelled at that, were a worse affront. Marmalade jars looked ugly enough when filled with flowers, he said, but when the flowers were blown away and the jars left absolutely empty it was an insult to the dead to label their resting place 'Keillers Dundee Marmalade!'

The problems of rural delinquency have been noted previously and the churchyard appears to have come in for more than its fair share of attention from the village vandals probably because, with the schoolyard opposite, it represented a convenient meeting place. There are many references to bad language and bad behaviour annoying those coming from the church. A letter to the *Western Gazette* in November 1889 stated:

> Sir, – Last Sunday evening, as I was passing by Bowerchalke church, I was surprised at the unruly conduct manifested outside the church as the congregation was leaving the sacred edifice, and on enquiring what it all meant, I was informed that it was caused by the idle young fellows who make a practice of congregating round the church gates but who do not attend the service. Even some of those who robe themselves in white surplices and take a prominent part in the services of the church, and who should be a pattern to the others, do not hesitate to join in their rowdy conduct, and do their part to annoy regular attendants at the church. . . .'
>
> *Western Gazette* 22 November 1889

A further cause for concern was the desecration of graves and damage to the churchyard wall. Stones were often thrown at the windows of adjacent houses and, on one occasion in 1889, a laurel hedge fringing the church was completely cut down leaving only the stumps of the bushes above ground. The offender was eventually identified and returned the stolen boughs making a public apology before the vicar and Sgt. Wallace, the local policeman, as a merciful alternative to prosecution, a course which would have meant imprisonment without the option of a fine.

Almost the first notice Collett ever printed in the *Parish Papers* was a list of rules he expected to be observed by the bellringers. Such an occupation appears to have carried prestige at that time and all members, (preferably communicants), were expected to have uncovered heads and to regard the occasion with due solemnity avoiding all needless talk and laughter. Bells were not to be used for purely secular enjoyment, although there were obviously exceptions to this rule through the years, and no payment apart from a 10*s*. charge at weddings, was to be received.

In 1880 the bells were re-hung on new timber frames, the cracked treble bell having been recast at Warners Bell Foundry in London. There are three bells in the tower which had been raised some 12ft. during the 1866 restoration. The treble bell is unmarked but the second, recast by John Wallis of Salisbury, is signed 'J.W. 1611' and the simple message 'Feare God' imprinted on it. The tenor bell, weighing 12cwt., has the words 'Ave Maria' engraved on it and an 'X', the sign of Roger Landon, a Wokingham founder at the end of the fifteenth century.

When the bells were restored, the new frame was designed and built for a fourth bell which would have produced a ring of twenty-four changes instead of six and Collett was very keen to do this in order to produce a sweeter sound. Moreover, in 1905 the bells were inspected by Mr J.R. Jerran, the Diocesan expert, whose report suggested that with a few alterations to the framework it would even be possible to have a fifth. Nothing was ever done to follow up these proposals, probably because the £70 needed to purchase and erect the new bells would have been a low priority compared with other requirements.

Trouble with the church roof continued after the 1879 deluge which flooded the chancel. Funds raised by parishioners in 1885 enabled Thomas Foyle to restore the ceiling with stained and varnished timber donated by Lord Pembroke. In August of the same year, however, another large piece of plaster fell during a communion service, luckily while the persons seated underneath were at the altar rail! The pulpit was a further casualty and on a third occasion plaster crashing onto the organ put it out of action for over a week. Periodic repairs were carried out but in 1913 leaks in the new south aisle compelled Thomas Foyle to strip the tiles and completely renovate the roof.

Heating was a further perennial problem (and still is!). In January 1885 Collett complained of the severe cold making it quite painful to be present and had the fires lit on Thursday in the hope of getting a breath of warm air by Sunday. There were constant complaints and all temporary repairs over the years proved ineffectual, so that a new heating system was installed in 1901, Jasper Elliott from Woodminton conveying the materials in his farm waggon from Salisbury.

The quality of church music was also a cause for concern. The new harmonium installed in 1866 was giving trouble by the time Collett arrived and in 1885 a small one was borrowed from the school. Fortune smiled at this time, for a lady of considerable means who had become engaged to a poor gentleman of musical tastes, had bought a new harmonium for him at a cost of £110. Later, the romance having turned sour, she broke off the engagement and allowed the church to have it for a third of its original price, an occurrence that led Collett to observe that matrimonial discords arise as well as musical ones. The sound, however, would probably have proved too thin for his growing congregation and four years later, when Broadchalke bought a new organ, the old one was purchased by Bowerchalke and placed in the north transept where it is still performing comparatively well today.

No vicar can survive long in his parish without a nucleus of committed supporters. Church offices, decided at the Easter Vestry Meeting underpinned the administration of the parish and raised the money needed to solve the kind of problems outlined above. William Wilkins, as Parish Clerk of long standing in the village and probably set in his ways could have given the new vicar a difficult time. Photographs in Collett's album, however, which show Wilkins as a grizzled old man in a patterned agricultural smock or in the surplice of senior chorister, indicate that they were good friends.

The Methodist Chapel (1888) recently converted into a house

When Wilkins retired aged eighty-five after twenty-seven years as Parish Clerk he was given a small pension by the Diocese but lived only a few months to enjoy it. Collett would have assumed many of his duties when he resigned as the post then ceased.

William Wilkins was not particularly wealthy. Nor was old Mrs Lawes, a washerwoman from Mead End who for many years washed all the choir surplices free of charge; in 1888 the choristers presented her with a canary bird as a token of their appreciation. John Coombs, local farmer and honey retailer, was one of the more prosperous members of the community. He lived at Binghams Farm and, later, at the Firs; both houses were of considerable size and antiquity, and he sat on many local committees as well as being churchwarden for a long period. His wife, Ellen, was also a tireless worker for the church, organising fund-raising events, arranging collections of items for the Infirmary and always giving generously of her time. Her gift of a hurricane lamp which enabled people to ascend the church steps at night in safety appears to have been of more use than the more elaborate wrought iron archway that later replaced it. The lamp on top of that was fine unless the weather happened to be windy when it often proved impossible to light!

The younger women who showed such interest in the new curate of 1878 may have had romantic aspirations and their assertiveness, perhaps competitiveness, were something of a strain to him. Nevertheless, without them his church would have been much the poorer. Laura Freeth and Maria Wood were spinsters of independent means whose gifts to the church are mentioned continually. Church ornaments and vestments, flowers in abundance for the festivals, subscriptions for new projects, all came readily from their pockets. In April 1889, for instance, Collett records thanks to Miss Freeth, 'for the gift of a quantity of beautiful hot house flowers for the decoration of the altar. She is also going to give us a pair of new banners, the work of her own hands.' The previous year she had donated two altar vases made from solid brass. Her generosity is more surprising when we consider that she was not even a permanent resident. She appears to have lived for some period at 2 St Pauls, Fisherton but was frequently recorded as resident in the Channel Islands. It was from Jersey in 1913, still remembering her friends in Bowerchalke despite recovering from a serious illness, that she sent a Christmas present of two large boxes of flowers for the church, sixpence and a card for each choirboy and threepence for every child in the school.

Maria Wood had her roots in the village. She was a person of some beauty to judge from Collett's photographs but she never married, living for much of her life in the little house at Misselfore that belonged to her parents. The white altar front was a gift from her and the windows of the south aisle were dedicated to her mother. Priscilla Aldwynkle, known to the schoolchildren as Polly, is first mentioned in the *Papers* as a temporary resident in 1908, giving dolls as prizes for the Sunday school treat. A tall, stately lady who wore her hair in a chignon style, she stayed to become a generous benefactor and a popular pianist at many social gatherings. For years she ran the children's Band of Mercy group, to instil in them a love of animals, and in 1910 in her home near the vicarage she ran classes for them to produce needlework, scrapbooks and other items as Christmas presents for the Infirmary.

John Linnell was the most dynamic and indispensable of all Edward Collett's helpers; his hand can be seen in just about every phase of church and village life. He came with the vicar in 1878 from his previous parish of Silverstone as a fourteen year-old boy. With him came Sarah Stone, a young girl who was to serve in the vicarage as housekeeper until her marriage to one of the wheelwright's sons, Edward Foyle, sixteen years later. Linnell had early aspirations towards the priesthood but the rustic existence at Bowerchalke obviously suited him too well. In his younger days he cut a dashing figure in the village; Collett's photographs show him in sporty cap and suit proudly displaying his penny farthing bicycle or in the uniform of the Bowerchalke Brass Band. Apart from a short period of eight years he remained in the village until his death at the age of ninety-seven, becoming involved in nearly every church job it is possible for a layman to do including verger and lay reader as well as organist for over half a century.

If this chapter has given the impression that Collett's church was a sombre institution devoted to little more than an unending succession of Sabbath day services, it has done him a grave disservice. There were summer fêtes and sales of work, evangelical missions and, of course, parties and outings – the most exciting events of the year for the younger members. The focus for these activities was the church choir and the Sunday school.

Sunday school classes, at 9.45 a.m. and 2 p.m. are both first mentioned in the *Papers* in 1884, but doubtless existed long before this. They were run at that time by Mrs Compton, the rather fierce-looking school mistress. Apathy existed even in those days, for in 1892 Collett reflected sadly, 'Sunday morning class closed for the present . . . not because we were tired of it or the dear little people themselves but only because, (with a very few exceptions), the parents are too lazy or indifferent to send their children!' Each child who was present before the bell stopped ringing received a ticket for attendance and another for learning the Collect. These were later exchanged for prizes according to a certain scale of values.

A Boot Club for the Sunday school pupils was another inducement to help poorer members and encourage thrift. Each Sunday afternoon Miss Wood collected their pennies and for every shilling collected a tuppenny bonus was added, the money being paid out for new boots or shoes each June and December.

It is difficult for us in the 1980s to understand the excitement which young people must have felt for the comparatively simple pleasures of life one hundred years ago before the advent of our sophisticated electronic society. Winter treats in particular must have been events eagerly anticipated by the children through the long winter days when money was scarce and other diversions so few. Collett's description of the Christmas party in 1884 reflects the merriment of such an occasion:

> THE CHRISTMAS TREE for the Sunday Scholars, was quite a new kind of treat for them, as hardly any of them had ever seen one before. It was given yesterday. The tree itself was the gift of Mr Challis, Head Gardener at Wilton and was a fine specimen, standing about 7 or 8 ft from the ground. It was kindly fetched from Wilton by one of Mr Elliott's carts. On its arrival, at about 3 o'clock it was fixed in the class room and was very soon decorated with a large variety of presents of all kinds and sizes, consisting of toys, garments, sweets, dolls etc. Many willing hands made short work and in an hour or two the tree looked like a bit of fairy land. At 6 o'clock refreshments were provided in the way of cake, bread and butter and coffee. After this followed games in which teachers and visitors seemed heartily to join, and at about 7.15 the lamps in the big room were put out and after a few moments of darkness, the door of the classroom was thrown open and the children trooped in to see for themselves the brightly illuminated and decorated tree. There was a hush of admiration, which gave way to louder expressions of satisfaction and merriment, as the children became possessors of the good things displayed before them. . . .
>
> *Parish Papers* 2 January 1885

In November 1889 it was games on the vicarage lawn followed by tea and, later in the evening, a magic lantern show to which all the children in the village were invited. Usually, the winter treat took place in the schoolroom where the tables could be moved together for tea and shifted aside afterwards for games. In 1906 a lucky sawdust tub was added to the usual romps and remained a great favourite for many years, every child being invited to dip their hand in twice and amidst great excitement they extracted a mystery gift. In 1907 came the phonograph adding further gaiety to the evening. Apart from the teachers, parents and any visitors to the parish were invited to join in the spirit of the party, usually bringing along mysterious parcels of their own. Such kind donations of food and gifts supplemented the half-yearly distribution of prizes for attendance and good work which were given out during the evening. In 1913, for example, when fifty-five scholars sat down to tea, four iced cakes were provided by Miss Freeth with a large number of prettily-packed chocolates in fancy baskets and vases for each child to which Miss Aldwynkle had added a

The wedding of the wheelwright's son Ted Foyle to Sarah Stone, the vicar's housekeeper

quantity of other presents. Books were also given to all and Miss Wood had previously given gifts of her own to the pupils in her class.

Although the vicar acted as the genial host on these occasions it was the organising ability of John Linnell that oiled the works. Similarly in the summer, all the preparations for the eagerly-awaited outings were left in his capable hands. It is interesting to note the effects of social change, particularly the improvements in transport, on the widening horizons of a community previously restricted to little more than the odd jaunt into Salisbury. In 1889 the children were content with a tea given by Miss Wood and her mother at their home at Misselfore and a few games in Mr Humby's adjoining meadow. The following year, conveyed in the carrier's van, the children were taken to the woody hamlet of Chase for a picnic. By 1903 they had crossed the downs to Pentridge where the *Salisbury Mirror* described a memorable day:

> SUMMER OUTING – Last Monday a most enjoyable treat was provided for the scholars of the Bowerchalke Sunday Classes. By the great kindness of the Revd A. & Mrs Poulton, the children and friends were invited to spend the afternoon and evening at Pentridge Rectory, which is about 3½ miles from Bowerchalke. A start was made at two o'clock. Mr Churchwarden Elliott of

> Woodminton Farm was so very good as to lend a large wagon and horses, which together with two brakes and a trap, conveyed the party very pleasantly and happily. The weather was fine, and the ride was most enjoyable. At 3.30 a short service was held in Pentridge Church, when after the singing of a hymn, the Rector spoke, dwelling briefly upon the idea of Church unity in the great Sacraments and in a common Faith. A move was then made to the Rectory meadow, where games were played till tea; this was served on the lawn, which had been decorated with banners, etc. After this games, races, and other amusements were enjoyed with unmistakable zest, and some music was kindly provided by a small band. At 8.30 the return journey was begun, but not until ringing cheers had been given to Mr and Mrs Poulton for their most hearty welcome and kindness.
>
> *Salisbury Mirror* 23 July 1903

On many occasions in this pre-mechanised era it was the kindness of local farmers, the Brachers, the Goldens and the Elliotts, who provided the simplest of amenities for the maximum of enjoyment – hot water and milk for tea, a daisy-studded field and a comfortable barn against the elements. At East Chase Farm, for example, along the winding road to Woodyates, the plantation of trees adjoining the house was a natural playground for children and the choirman, Walter Bracher, with his young wife, often held the outing there:

> SUNDAY CLASSES TREAT at East Chase Farm in large field opposite the Farmhouse. Soon after 2 the children were ready to start and younger ones had a lift in Mr Vincent's waggon which carried the provisions and crockery. Mrs W. Bracher was waiting to welcome us with a smiling face and kindly words. . . . Swings in the trees, see saws across the fallen trunks, gambols and races in the field all helped to pass away the time til tea in the barn. Willing helpers had been busy while the younger ones had been at play and when the signal given the meal began. At the close one of the guests Miss Mary Humby of Christchurch gave two amusing recitations in Wiltshire dialect. . . .
>
> *Parish Papers* 30 July 1908

By 1911, the village was becoming bolder in its choice of venue; for the next two years there were visits to the Larmer Tree Gardens, the magnificent pleasure grounds created by General Pitt-Rivers on his estate near Tollard Royal, which attracted thousands of visitors during the 1890s and early twentieth century. On a beautiful July day the children and teachers, accompanied by nearly forty friends and neighbours, met at the vicarage at 11.30 a.m. to make the nine-mile journey in six large brakes and vans. It must have looked like a pioneering venture. As the roads were hilly there was a good deal of walking at intervals in order to rest the horses and a halt was made at Sixpenny Handley to witness a decorated procession making its way to a flower show. When they reached the grounds there was plenty to see: the Temple, the Oriental Buildings and, of course, the ancient wych-elm after which the gardens were named. German skittles, bowls and swingboats were available in the shrubbery and a menagerie of the General's exotic animals and birds, all a novel experience for the saucer-eyed children. At 4 o'clock tea was served in a large hall, 'everything beautifully clean and orderly'. For the next two hours they played games and explored the vast grounds at will before departing at 7.30 p.m. after a day that many of them would never forget.

By 1912 Robert Williamson, farmer and watercress grower at Knowle Farm, had added a motor coach to his expanding interests which provided the first regular motorised service into Salisbury and in the following year advantage was taken of this to take the choir, and then the Sunday school, for their first-ever venture to the seaside. In the 'brightest and most beautiful of summer weather', and through generous donations from friends, the party was taken in the village bus with an additional charabanc from Shrewton on the 2½-hour journey to Bournemouth. At the pier the children were supplied with light refreshments while they gazed with indescribable pleasure for the first time at the sea. They played on the sands, rode donkeys and explored the town while some of the more adventurous enjoyed a sea trip to Swanage. At 5 o'clock they assembled for tea at the Tregonwell Restaurant before returning wearily to Bowerchalke by 9.45 p.m.

In 1914 this venture was successfully repeated but the dark clouds of war were beginning to overshadow even so remote a spot as Bowerchalke. For the next few years it was back to Salisbury Race Plain or the Elliott's Farm at Woodminton where, despite rationing in the latter phase of the war, a tea for the children was somehow always managed. It took a little while for normality to be restored but by 1921, with the aid of the bus and Mr Beckley's lorry, excited youngsters were once more enjoying the salty air of Bournemouth.

Similar events were enjoyed by the choir. As early as 1880 a visit was paid to the village of Britford, near Salisbury, for a cricket match against the choir there. A pleasant day of sport ended with a church service: 'The singing was hearty and effective, and was rendered in a way which went far to prove that the service was not the least enjoyable part of the day's holiday.' There were similar trips recorded in the 1900s involving Hindon. Later, when many of Collett's first generation of choirboys had grown into manhood, the highlight of the year became the Choirmen's Supper and Social, with a tea for the boys. The teas were usually in the home of one or other of the village worthies. This must have been quite a tight fit; in 1912, Miss Aldwynkle in her rented cottage near the vicarage, had her party in two halves on successive evenings in order to get them all in.

The Choirmen's Suppers in the schoolroom were much grander affairs, the redoubtable John Linnell once more proving an efficient and enthusiastic

The interior of Bowerchalke Church showing the altar decorated for the Harvest Festival, 1884

organiser, with Miss Wood usually providing the finance. Often, the sons of the local farmers such as John B. Coombs from 'The Firs' and Claude Williamson, son of the watercress grower, were invited with others from the surrounding area. A meal of roast beef, ham and vegetables was enjoyed, with Linnell usually doing the carving, followed by a steaming plum pudding, mince pies and cheese. The rest of the evening would be spent very pleasantly with the assembled gathering joining in games, singing and dancing accompanied by 'Polly' Aldwynkle on the piano or, before her arrival, by Bill Gatehouse's gramophone.

A regular visitor to the vicarage throughout Collett's life was his elder brother John. He loved the village and had many friends there. For twenty-five years he was priest-in-charge of Worplesdon-cum-Burpham, near Guildford but spent his holidays in Bowerchalke preaching regularly and taking part in all its activities. In 1910, when he was 'thrown down by a motor', sustaining cuts, bruises and several broken ribs, regular bulletins as to his progress were given in the *Parish Papers* to allay anxious enquiries. He was a dark, thick-set man with a dense black beard. Mrs Greta Case describes him as totally different from his brother: 'he was a nice man but we liked our own the best.' In 1913 he resigned his parish and moved to Teffont Magna across the downs from Bowerchalke in the Nadder Valley. Frank Golden, a young boy from the village who was later killed in the First World War, left to go into service with him, but regularly trundled over with messages from him or to bring John's magic lantern strapped to his bicycle.

When John retired from Teffont he went to live at Glen Cairn, the house near the vicarage previously rented by Miss Aldwynkle. There, in 1924, when Edward Collett died, he was joined by John Linnell who had to leave the vicarage. John Collett died shortly after, but Linnell continued his active involvement in the village though now in his early sixties. Upon the death of his estranged first wife, he married Annie Habgood, whose family had managed the Bell Inn for generations. The church had a new encumbant now and was adapting its ways accordingly but for the next thirty-seven years Linnell continued to serve it as organist and lay reader until his own death at ninety-seven in 1961.

5
The Children

DEATH OF MRS WILKINS – Mrs Jane Wilkins died on the 25th ult. aged 75. For fifty years she had worked in the cause of education and she kept the village school for a long period before any scheme of Government education existed. For ten years in the latter part of her life Mrs Wilkins walked six miles a day in all weathers to superintend the Chase School: but some time before her death her daughter took her place. Mrs Wilkins' remains were buried on Sunday in the village churchyard.

Salisbury Journal Saturday 8 July 1882

When it is fine and the atmosphere clear you can see from parts of the Chase right across the chequered Dorset countryside to the Solent but for much of the year the south-westerly gales or the biting cold from the north must have made for a hardier breed than the valley people. Today not a trace of the tiny Chase School remains except in the memories of a few. Situated in Stanchill Wood, it was established by the Earl of Pembroke in 1869 as a dame school to provide a simple education for the children of labourers living in some fifteen isolated cottages at East, Middle and West Chase Farms and Stermal Gate near Handley. Twelve pupils attended the opening of the school, each of whom paid a fee of one penny a week.

Mrs Jane Wilkins, wife of the Parish Clerk, lived in a cottage in Quidham Street and must have been very dedicated to undertake such a steep and exposed journey all those years. This was when, to use Collett's words, 'schools were free from state tyranny and working people's children were not forced to learn ten thousand times more than is good for them.' Certainly the education received at Chase would have been very rudimentary indeed for the building was small and the resources practically non-existent.

Mrs Wilkins' daughter, also named Jane, had an illegitimate child by John Elliott, the younger son of one of Bowerchalke's most prominent farmers. Presumably because of the disgrace, he was sent away to work near Blandford and it is surprising that with Victorian insistence on at least outward moral respectability she was allowed to take over her mother's work; even so, the life of a one-parent family at that time would have been considerably more difficult than that of today. A small woman with rather

Stanley Wilkins with his mother, 1884

swarthy features and severely parted jet black hair, she appears to have done it with the same dedication as her mother and was much respected. Her work, in cramped conditions and hampered by lack of facilities, was carried out uncomplainingly. However, some help was provided by a donation of £3 from Lord Pembroke in 1885 and a further £1 7*s.* 7½*d.* from a village event which were used to provide books and furniture as well as to carry out urgent repairs.

The school was also used as a meeting place for the few inhabitants of the scattered community. A weekly service was conducted there for a while by the vicar and baptisms recorded in 1888 and 1889. In the latter year a tea and entertainment, organised by Miss Wilkins, took place when, despite the large crowd hemmed in and the great warmth of the evening, a most enjoyable time was had, three hearty cheers being given at the end for 'the excellent management of the painstaking headmistress.'

In the summer holidays of that year, however, Miss Wilkins resigned and a small advertisement was placed in the *Church Times*:

£10 A YEAR and unfurnished cottage offered to communicant, who will teach a

> tiny dame school (non-Government) in a little hamlet, two miles from the church – Apply Vicar of Bowerchalke, Salisbury.

A replacement was not easy to find and for a while the school was closed, the children presumably travelling to the National School in the village. It re-opened on 1 December under Mrs Inez Muller at an earlier time of 9 a.m. instead of 10 a.m. with hopes expressed by the vicar that it might soon come under official control with a yearly inspection like the school in the village. The school house had been papered and re-decorated in preparation for her arrival and Mrs Muller appears to have made quite an impression in the short time she was there. As to her teaching abilities there is no record, but the concert she arranged within a few weeks of her arrival was enjoyed by the village friends and Chase neighbours who crowded into the school house. Not least among her admirers was John Linnell who used to bring her down to the church in a pony and trap. Her husband, somewhat older than her, was a sick man on his arrival and died in the following April. Fifteen months later she resigned to marry Linnell and together they left the area. The loss of his protégé must have come as a great shock to the vicar despite Linnell's popularity with the ladies. However, the marriage was not a success and eight years later, Mrs Linnell departed for Australia with their two daughters leaving her husband to return to the vicarage.

The Chase School was once more without a teacher and the occasion seems to have led to something of a rift between Collett and Lord Pembroke. The Earl requested that the vicar make an appointment expressing the wish that, if possible, the new teacher should be one of the cottagers from the Chase. Reluctantly, Collett appointed Clara Patten, daughter of the Earl's carter, who had no teaching experience whatsoever. He made the appointment a probationary one, informing the Earl that he would leave the final decision to him and would no longer recognise the Chase as a parish school. Although no further mention is made of it in the *Parish Papers*, Clara Patten appears to have continued for some years until its closure in 1897 when the children were forced to walk the long and exposed journey to the village school, for some, well over two miles. Kate Golden, for example, from Middle Chase Farm whose elder sister had attended the Chase School, had to travel over this distance along muddy tracks to reach the National School in the village; Augustus Foyle at West Chase Farm had a journey of over three miles. The Foyles were more fortunate, however, having a pony and trap which they often used to transport the children to the village. Kate remembers when several of them begged a lift. There were six on the trap that morning and the axle broke. After that Augustus travelled to school on horseback!

There is no record as far as I can ascertain of the date the parish school was built, although Collett's estimate of 1844 seems fairly accurate as it was then that Lord Pembroke donated land opposite the church for that purpose. The first school Log Book was mislaid in the last century and cannot, therefore, confirm this but a previous Diocesan Inspector of the school, Archdeacon Lear, in correspondence with Collett, confirms the date: 'I have found in the records of the Board of Education that in 1844 a grant of £15 was made towards a school in Bowerchalke. I remember examining the school in 1847.' Originally, it possessed a galleried hall with no separate classroom, although one was added later for the infants. There was no residence for the teacher until much later in 1874 and the playground was little more than meadow land surrounded by a rough hedge which the older pupils were regularly caned for climbing!

The loss of that first Log Book is unfortunate as little is recorded elsewhere of those early days. The Revd Lutt, a previous curate of the parish wrote, 'When I went to Bowerchalke, [1859], there was an elderly woman as mistress, whose name I think was Barrett. Shortly after I became curate I obtained a very good mistress from the Salisbury Training College, a Miss Green, who was there when we left in 1862.' Subsequent history can be deduced from three sources: the *Parish Papers*, the surviving School Log Books which commence in 1875 and the Inspectors' reports referred to in both. These are supplemented at a later stage by the memories of those pupils, still living and traceable, who were educated there.

Not surprisingly, for so small and remote a school, there were many problems to contend with. Sickness, wilful truancy, exposure to the capriciousness of the English weather, childhood employment to eke out subsistence wages, all tended to deplete attendance and retard educational progress. There were many complaints by the Inspectors of overcrowding and cold, damp conditions with very poor ventilation. Lack of enthusiasm from parents who had received little education themselves and could see no reason why their children should be taken from gainful employment in the fields was often reflected in the pupils themselves who were dull and unforthcoming in their responses. The fee of one penny per week, obligatory until education was provided free of charge in 1891, must also have been a disincentive to many cottagers. (In the neighbouring village of Broadchalke, the Log Book indicates a rising scale of charges: 1*d.* for labourers, 2*d.* for artisans, 3*d.* for farmers.) It is little wonder that with these problems to contend with the calibre of the teaching staff was often poor and that many, assisted in the main by no more than an inexperienced monitoress, remained only for relatively short periods.

The first Inspector's Report in the Log Book, that of February 1875, set the tone for many a discouraging entry: 'My Lords have taken into consideration the Mistress's illness during part of the past school year and have allowed an unreduced grant to be paid, notwithstanding the poor results obtained at the examination in Arithmetic. A better report will be

Boys from the National School in 1884. The headmistress, Mrs Compton, is on the left

looked for next year.' But by next year that mistress had gone and a new one, Maria Furnice, assisted by her monitoress, Jane Williams, had made valiant attempts to raise the achievement levels.

Sickness sometimes closed the school for long periods of time on the instruction of the Medical Officer; measles, whooping cough, chickenpox and influenza being the main offenders. Smaller, but just as worrying, must have been the outbreaks of diphtheria, impetigo, scabies and 'unclean heads'. Entries such as 'not a good attendance today on account of the wet weather' are legion,' inclement weather must have been a sore trial to parents when drying facilities in homes were practically non-existent.

The Revised Code of 1862 controlled the conditions under which Government grants were to be paid. They were awarded to the school managers on the basis of regular attendance at school and a satisfactory report from the School Inspector at the annual examination – hence the preoccupation in the school Logs with statistics of weekly attendance. It must have been a discouraging battle. Potato planting in April, haymaking, gleaning after the harvest, nutting and potato picking in October were the main causes of truancy happily abetted by parents; there were many others. Typical of the frustrations experienced by rural teachers, was the entry of 19 June 1876: 'A very poor attendance especially in the upper classes. The children being taken by the parents into the fields haymaking.' This is followed by an entry for the 10–15 June: 'The whole of the week the attendance has been very thin, some of the children haymaking, others kept at home to take charge of the younger children while their parents go to work.' On 18 September, following the Harvest Holiday: 'School opened this morning but closed again this afternoon the attendance being so small in consequence of the Harvest not being completed. The attendance in the morning 5, afternoon 4.' Small numbers like this often led to the registers being closed and the rest of the children being sent home, presumably so that the poor attendance would not then be set against the school's grant.

Activities in connection with Club Day were often spread either side of the main occasion to such an extent that the Whitsun holiday – usually taken by many unofficially – became a fixture. Many other entries in the Log indicate the indifference of parents, hard-pressed by the domestic necessities of a large family and financial hardship, to the educational requirements of the law. Items like 'gone to Broadchalke for medicine' or 'several infants left for the winter' supplement further agricultural intrusions for apple and strawberry picking or just gardening in general.

Maria Furnice remained at her post for nearly three years and was there to welcome Edward Collett in 1878. Despite her efforts the Inspector was not impressed and in the following year recorded:

> The results of the examination show a decided falling off, and in Arithmetic to the marked extent of 36% with the exception of that of the first standard, no part of the work under this head is satisfactory. The Reading and Writing of the second standard are only pretty fair, and Reading of the third standard but moderate. The elder infants are backward. My Lords will look for decidedly better results in Arithmetic next year.

Collett was quick to come to the mistress's defence and wrote in the Log:

> The above report being manifestly unfair I have written to the Department asking a second Examination, and complaining that the Examiner frightened the children out of all they knew by his severity and his hard questions. I enter this here in fairness to the Mistress, who has deserved a far better Report.

Maria Furnice, however, had had enough and resigned the following day.

The new teacher in March 1879, Robert McAlpine, was unqualified but intended to sit for his certificate at Christmas. To enable him to do this the inspectorate paid a special visit to the school in October but owing to the unfavourable results, a letter was sent to the vicar, who acted as School Correspondent, in which it was stated that Mr McAlpine would no longer be allowed to sit his examination. Furthermore, no grant could be made to the school so long as it remained in the charge of an uncertificated teacher.

This was one more example of the inflexible and unsympathetic nature of the inspectorate at that time and Collett had no alternative but to accept McAlpine's resignation. In a subsequent letter, the schoolmaster expressed his belief that if the inspection had not occurred immediately after the Harvest Holidays (six weeks) and if the Inspector had not examined the school 'as though a year had elapsed' he would have succeeded better – not an unreasonable comment. Nevertheless, the 1881 Census Returns show that two years later Robert McAlpine was still residing in the village presumably unable to obtain a post.

Miss Eliza Waite, appointed in 1880, left after a year to marry one of the many visitors who accompanied the vicar on his daily visit to the school to conduct prayers and instruct the older pupils in the Catechism. Within 1881 the school was to have three successive headteachers and the results, as the Inspector was quick to point out, were correspondingly poor. In 1883, the principal teacher, William Kendall, was told that he, too, could not be issued with a certificate until better results were obtained in Arithmetic.

Mrs Caroline Compton who arrived in November of that year was a small bird-like person who used her own interpretation of the new Education Code to enforce her discipline:

1 Any child who comes to school late, will be kept in after the others have been dismissed, and will have a lesson to do.

2 A child is considered late who is not in school by the time the bell stops.

3 Any child attending with dirty hands, face, or clothes, or with uncombed hair will be punished.

One cause of lateness was the resentment of Dissenters to the denominational instruction given in the early part of the morning by the new vicar Some of the bolder spirits withdrew their children from such lessons as shown by an entry of 1883: 'By desire of their father, William and Edward Hardiman are henceforth withdrawn from all Religious Instruction' and again in 1884: 'By desire of their father, Albert, William and Florence Lawson are henceforth withdrawn from Religious Instruction.' Many, however, simply voted with their feet by turning up late to such an extent that for a while secular instruction was commenced immediately after 9 o'clock, prayers and the religious instruction were then taught at 11.15 a.m. This was discontinued after the next inspection so that in 1904 Collett was still protesting:

> A stranger visiting the school at 9 o'clock in the morning and during the time of religious instruction would very reasonably imagine that he had come to a

The National School with its recently added school house, 1884

> parish where God's Name was unknown to the parents of the children if he judged by the few of those who attended.
>
> *Parish Papers* 23 June 1904

In this respect Collett was being less than fair to the Dissenters whose objections were certainly not based upon grounds of indifference. Further evidence of their point of view was clearly illustrated in the *Salisbury Times* of 19 September 1902 following a meeting of the local Baptist Association at Bowerchalke. Reference was made to the statistics from Bowerchalke Parish School taken from the annual Blue Book of the Education Department, and grave concern was expressed that the school, which derived nearly all its income from public funds, was managed entirely by 'a public committee consisting of the vicar, his two churchwardens and two farmers of the district, the vicar being the central and by far the most prominent figure.' They clearly objected to their children being in the care of 'this sacrament-loving vicar'.

Mrs Compton's main problem, however, remained one of getting the children to attend school at all. A letter to the Managers from the Board of Guardians said, 'The Notices to the parents at Bowerchalke for non-attendance of children at school seem to be legion', a complaint which Edward Collett took up in the *Parish Papers*:

> . . . It really only wants a little management, as may be seen from the fact that there are some children who hardly ever miss, and yet whose home duties are as urgent as anyone's; while often enough on the other hand, those children who have little to do at home are the most frequent away from school.

A little harsh, perhaps, but Collett was well aware of the effect on the Annual Grant of a low average attendance. Worst of all the offenders was Henry Sellwood. His grandmother, who tried to bring him up, found him quite beyond her control. She was unable to get him to school despite numerous visits from the Attendance Officer and his name appears many times in the Log until eventually he was sent away to a reformatory.

There were, of course, many legitimate opportunities for the children to be away. Records of half-day and even whole-day holidays sprinkle the Log pages liberally. Both the church and the chapel took their annual treats on a week day. Holy days, such as Ascension, Ash Wednesday and the Feast of St Barnabas were often taken; on Good Friday and Easter Monday the attendance was so poor that a holiday gradually became accepted as the only reasonable course. Then there were local occasions such as the Potato and, later, the Flower Shows, parish teas and concerts, all of which required the schoolroom as their only large indoor area for communal activity. Occasionally time would be given for attendance at the funeral of a scholar such as Lizzie Penny in 1892. The annual Government Examination and Diocesan Inspections were both daunting experiences to be followed by a half-day's holiday and Empire Day, an occasion for much jingoistic tub-thumping, meant a half-day preceded by lessons on colonial expansion, the singing of patriotic songs and the saluting of the flag in the schoolyard.

Despite her diminutive appearance, Mrs Compton was a hard worker and not slow to wield the cane or even to expel for disobedience in order to enforce her discipline. Following the 1883 inspection the school was supplied with six new convertible desks, new reading books, slates and other apparatus to assist her efforts. The school treat in the following July is also evidence of a good spirit at this time when, despite the dismal weather, the children joined those at the Chase for their annual outing:

> THE SCHOOL TREAT has been quite the event of the past week, to which many little people had been looking forward for some weeks past. It was therefore with great disappointment that they saw it was likely to prove a wet day, an expectation which was fully verified by the continuance of heavy showers of rain. The start from Bowerchalke took place during an interval of fine weather, but the scene at the Chase, at about four o'clock was a trifle dismal, for the rain was falling as liberally as though it thought there was no other water to make the tea of, while the children were huddling together under every available shelter. By and bye, however, it cleared up, and after an abundantly furnished meal, the children entered fully into the games, races etc which were provided for them. Some books, toys, Useful things (such as

socks, collars, and handkerchiefs), were given away, together with sweets and fruit, all of which things were either presented by the parishioners or else purchased out of the money contributed by them and by other friends. At 8 o'clock the waggons began to reload, and it was not long before the village resounded with merry shouts and with the less tuneful sounds of the penny trumpets, mouth organs, and a variety of other 'musical instruments', the sweetness of whose strains is such as to make one feel glad they are only made up in penn'orths at a time. The management of this treat – Mrs Compton for the Village scholars, and Miss Wilkins for the Chase ones, have asked us to publicly express sincere gratitude for all the kind help. . . .

Parish Papers 26 July 1884

In September 1885, Mrs Compton resigned from the school as her husband had obtained a position in London. In subsequent years the Comptons fell on hard times as entries in the *Parish Papers* indicate:

AN URGENT APPEAL We are sorry to hear from our old friend Mrs Compton that she and her family are in very grievous distress. She has asked us to make an appeal to those who remember her, as well as to her former pupils to relieve her in her present troubles. It appears that her husband has had no regular employment for six months and for the last seven weeks has been unable to get any work at all. Besides this her eldest boy is out of a situation and two children are ill with bronchitis. Mrs Compton adds 'During the

Robert Williamson's two young sons, 1889. Williamson was a farmer and watercress grower

> whole of the last week we had to live on bread only. We have disposed of everything we can possibly do without . . . I am writing now to ask you if you will kindly take interest in our sad case and ask a few friends and the school children I once knew at Bowerchalke if they would kindly give a trifle each to help us in our desperate need'.
>
> *Parish Papers* 29 November 1888

Help was forthcoming from the village but, much later in 1908 there was a further appeal for help as they were in abject poverty, Mr Compton had been unemployed for two years and their children sent away. But this time her pupils had grown up; memories had diminished and the response was less positive.

For a few months after Mrs Compton left, the school was taken over by Thomas Lloyd, a highly recommended schoolmaster from Welshpool. His wife took the sewing classes and his daughter became monitoress to the infants. The Log Book entries reflect a professional, caring and critical attitude at this time. Nor was Mr Lloyd frightened to take on the farmers for their cynical misuse of their labourers' children; 'George Chalk absent working for Mr Harding, Farmer – this boy is only 10 years of age, and the above farmer persists in engaging the boy after my warning him of the consequences (School Log January 1886).' It was to little avail as subsequent entries prove, a particularly poor attitude when one considers that Mr Harding was one of the school managers. The highlight of Mr Lloyd's time was the visit to the village, described earlier, of John Wordsworth, the new Bishop of Salisbury, who distributed the shillings and sixpences given annually to children who had passed the examination in either two or three subjects. Sadly, after a few months, Mr Lloyd retired with his family to Canada to be near his son, an event the village seems genuinely to have regretted, a generous subscription being raised on his behalf.

Mr James Caddy, the new master, was to remain for twenty-three years, well into living memory. Accompanied by his sister Emily who took the infants, and a succession of monitoresses including two of the wheelwright's daughters, he helped bring a period of stability that the school needed, though his teaching appears unexciting and the difficulties he encountered made the period a stressful one. The children remained 'dull, slow in answering' and attempts to start a night class were not very fruitful. Nevertheless, the Inspector's report of 1887 cautiously expressed that some progress had been made:

> The school is in good order and a very creditable progress has been made in arithmetic. The first standard is still backward and spelling needs attention in the third standard. A promising beginning has been made in Grammar but the knowledge of the children is moderate at present.

Subsequent reports refer to a fairly low level of progress despite this promising start, with insufficient warmth in the infants' room, lack of ventilation and the need for a proper urinal. The schoolyard resembled a ploughed field in wet weather until the school treasurer, Charles Elliott, purchased some Fordingbridge red gravel which was carried by Mr Stevens' traction engine to make some attempt at restitution.

In 1891 came the new Act which at last made education free to all children. It remained difficult to enforce attendance, however, anxiety over the high rate of truancy continued and frequent visits from the Attendance Officer proved to be of little avail. Nor was the new Act universally popular. Collett, steeped in many of the prejudices and traditions of his day objected strongly to this 'pauperising bill' as he called it:

> . . . We notice in the parliamentary reports, that it is intended after the first day of next September to provide free education in all our parish schools throughout England. In other words parents are to be deprived by law of the privilege of providing for the education of their own children! It conveys the idea that the government look upon the people either as a nation of paupers who cannot afford to pay a penny a week per child or else as a nation of noodles who have not got moral courage enough to take care that their children learn to read and write! We should have thought such a provision would have been too humiliating to have been borne by a people considering themselves an 'independent' race. We are, by no means forgetful of the comparatively few who really are too poor to pay: for to such as they, education is already free, so that there is no grievance to be removed. We fancy that all upright people will agree in thinking that those who can pay should pay and that Free Education is servile, unnatural and absurd and its introduction amongst the lower classes, little short of an insult.
>
> *Parish Papers* 30 April 1891

No doubt, he observed wryly in a subsequent edition, it would be warmly applauded by those parents who already shirk nearly all their other responsibilities towards their families.

Even before the passing of this Act, numbers on the school register had increased dramatically. One hundred names were on roll in 1891 with an average attendance of eighty-four as opposed to numbers of about fifty a few years earlier. Although this led to higher grants, overcrowding was particularly evident in the infants' class where children were forced to sit three at a desk or on boxes and the fragile progress observed earlier was once more arrested. The Inspector in the following year stated:

> I regret to report that the elementary work this year is very unsatisfactory and that the condition of the school is one of inefficiency. . . . The grant has not been withheld for the past year but formal warning is now given that it may be withheld at the next inspection if H.M. Inspector again reports the school as inefficient.

During the following two years this threat was carried out; the grant was withheld thus depriving the school of resources at the very time that support and encouragement were most needed. Following a further series of inspections when the school remained clearly too full and understaffed for effective teaching, the withholding of grants and the threat of a formal warning were again given in the early 1900s.

The dullness of the children would have been partly due to the absence of any cultural stimulus at home rather than lack of innate ability. Following the poor report of 1905 Collett used the argument below in his efforts to support the hard-pressed teachers:

> School was visited last tuesday by H.M.I. Mr Hodson who spent the greater part of the day in examining the children. Unfortunately the weather was very dismal and this circumstance was likely to have had its effect on them in making their answers somewhat less bright than they might otherwise have been. We thank Mr Hodson for the pains he took and we are sure he will send us a faithful report in due time. He seemed much impressed by the fact that while the children knew the lessons which they had been taught, their way of answering was so stolid and lifeless. We quite agree with him. From some of them it is hard work to get so much as a smile. But, poor little things, in many a home they get precious little encouragement to smile! And life – with the Smile left out of it – is not worth calling Life.
>
> *Parish Papers* 7 December 1905

There is no doubt, too, that the fear of lost grants forced many schools to concentrate narrowly on sewing and the '3 Rs' to the exclusion of a broader and more stimulating curriculum. The comment in a report, for example, 'Knitting is required to be taught if they wish to obtain a grant for boys' needlework', would hardly have impressed the sons of agricultural labourers who formed the majority of Bowerchalke school at this time. Nor, I suspect, would Caddy's object lessons on 'the carrot' or the 'earwig'! Collett's remarks on this narrowness show particular insight:

> The word 'educate' means to lead out. But the Government interpretation of the same word is to force in! The consequence of this official blunder is that the much vaunted education of this country is more or less of a failure. It is not the Teachers' fault that when nine tenths of the children leave school they cannot read intelligently and with proper expression; or even write a gracefully worded letter to their friends; or shew forth the result of their education in their manners. And this is simply because of cramming their brains with needless learning, in order to gain higher Grants. It is as cruel as it is foolish and helps greatly to fill our lunatic asylums with inmates. . . .
>
> *Parish Papers* 14 August 1902

Gradually, with the establishment of the Board of Education in 1899 and the 1902 Education Act which placed education in the hands of local authorities, attitudes became more compassionate. Annual inspections disappeared and the role of the Inspector, so long feared as a stern and unfeeling instrument of government, became that of adviser. This is clearly demonstrated by the reports, which became briefer and more encouraging in tone. Reports in the *Parish Papers*, too, reflected this brevity:

> THE SCHOOL was visited and examined yesterday afternoon by H.M. Assistant Inspector Mr Bond who expressed his satisfaction at the marked improvement for which he complimented Mr Caddy and the teachers. This is very encouraging for future effort.
>
> *Parish Papers* 14 November 1907

In the following February, the same Inspector made an alteration in the position and arrangement of the desks so that the scholars would not sit with their backs to the light.

Reports on Religious Instruction in the school, which continued long after the government ones, were carried out by the rural dean as a representative of the Diocese of Salisbury. These were always gentler in tone and more sensitive to the problems of the teachers. Less formal, but probably as awesome to the children were the annual visits from Lady Pembroke, usually accompanied by her daughter and one or two of the ladies of the village such as Mrs Coombs or Miss Wood, to present prizes. These were for good conduct, regular attendance and needlework and usually consisted of books. Other prizes of baskets, workboxes and purses are mentioned as being given by teachers or village notables.

The annual winter party would have been eagerly looked forward to as an escape from the dull routine – probably as much by the staff as the children. This account from the *Parish Papers* in 1893 would have been fairly typical:

> The treat passed off very pleasantly indeed, all the arrangements being carried out most successfully by Mr and Miss Caddy and numerous willing helpers. We were sorry that the prevailing sickness kept a good many children at home as we all should have liked everyone of them to be present. The treat began at 5 with a plentiful tea followed by the giving away of presents each scholar receiving something useful. Then came the magic Lantern in which were shewn the stories of Little Red Riding Hood, The Tiger and the Tub and the Sweep and the Whitewasher, besides some dozens of comical moveable pictures. . . .
>
> *Parish Papers* 16 February 1893

At Christmas there would be gifts of toy puzzles, card games and yard measures, (sent on one occasion by the proprietors of Holloways Pills), and a Christmas tree to grace their festivities. At Whitsun, Isaac Sheppard, that most generous of village benefactors, returned from his successful London business to join the Club Feast Day celebrations and always stopped by to

The school children of Bowerchalke in 1904

hear the children sing before presenting them with buns and oranges. Another regular and popular visitor was the entertainer George Foote whose vocal imitations of musical instruments and the comic contortions of his face caused endless merriment. Under the title of 'Foote's Funny Fancies' he returned again and again to the delight of the children and, it has to be said, to the vicar!

An impression of school life at that time is related by Greta Case who, as Greta Penny was the daughter of Mr Williamson's head shepherd:

> *Edward Collett was the vicar here when I started school at five and he was here right through my schooling. With his black surplice and black hat he came to school every morning at 9 o'clock for prayers after a hymn. Mr Caddy and his sister were there then. He was a nice schoolmaster but had trouble with the older ones. They could be very troublesome and awkward. Mr Caddy wanted my husband to stay beyond 12 years and study to be a schoolmaster, too, but he would have none of it. He wanted to work on the land; he did and did it well. When things got out of hand in the class room, Mr Caddy sent a boy for Mr Collett and he came over and calmed things down.*

In February 1909 James Caddy resigned, exhausted and in very poor health. He left the schoolhouse where he had lived for nearly twenty-three years and took up abode in 'Hillview', the little cottage opposite the vicarage where Thomas Foyle, the wheelwright and carpenter had raised his large family. A quiet, modest man, remembered with affection by those ex-scholars I have spoken with, James Caddy requested that no testimonial should be raised for him. The village, however, was appreciative of his efforts to educate their young, often against enormous odds, and a collection was arranged. One old scholar, Harry Bruton, wrote to the vicar:

> How very sorry I was to hear of Mr Caddy resigning owing to ill health. When I was under him he did all his best to try and get me on. Yes sir, I honoured him very much. I found him a very good natured master. . . . I dare say you are thinking of giving him a farewell gift so I have enclosed 1 shilling so I shall be numbered among the subscribers. So I hope you will do your best sir, in collecting for Mr Caddy as he is an old friend of mine and everybody else.

Mr Caddy was not able to enjoy his premature retirement. Although only forty-five, he died within two months of his resignation. The children readily brought their pennies to buy flowers for his grave and a more lasting tribute was placed in the form of a marble cross at his grave given by old scholars of the school.

The scene was now set for the emergence of a personality of an entirely different ilk – though not without a constitutional battle between the school managers and the local education authority. Thomas Hyde Penfound had previously been assistant master at St Martins Boys' School in Salisbury. Appointed with some haste in a temporary capacity due to Mr Caddy's illness, he made a good impression with the school managers who wished to confirm him in his position:

> At a meeting of the school managers which was held last Saturday evening to consider appointment of new Head Teacher the name of Mr Thomas Hyde Penfound was proposed by the vicar and seconded by Mr Harding and he has therefore been formally nominated subject to the approval and sanction of the County Council Board of Education. There were about 30 or more applicants for the post but the preference was given to Mr Penfound because of his good success with the children during his temporary engagement.
>
> *Parish Papers* 4 March 1909

The County Council, however, opposed this appointment:

> The School continues to improve under the successful teaching and discipline of Mr Penfound who it will be remembered was appointed Head master by the managers on February 27. The County Council has opposed this and is in favour of a Mistress. This we strongly object to and will do our best to prevent. It would seem an absurdity to have any managers at all, if their decision can be set aside by a committee which has no personal knowledge whatever of the local circumstances! Managers, Parents and children are all

unanimous in wishing Mr Penfound to remain and (if need be) will make an appeal against the despotic action of the council.

Parish Papers 22 April 1909

A classic example, one might say, as to where the power lies. The Education Committee continued to adhere to the opinion that a mistress should be appointed, but by June yielding to the strong representations of the managers, sanctioned Mr Penfound's appointment until the end of the year, although leaving his permanent engagement subject to an Inspector's report. This proved satisfactory and his position was finally confirmed at a salary of £90 per annum allowing him to move into the schoolhouse with his mother and sister.

Thomas Penfound was a strong disciplinarian who made his position clear from the beginning as the School Log Book shows:

There was a (seemingly) organised attempt on the part of six of the older boys to be insubordinate today. I at once took the matter in hand and settled it definitely. I regret it was necessary to promptly punish the two chief offenders, I feel sure, however, that when I get to know the boys better and they me we shall get on quite amicably and smoothly together.

School Log Book 8 February 1909

From the beginning he adopted a surprisingly modern approach to his teaching making it practical rather than theoretical and applying the knowledge they acquired to the purposes of their everyday life. On fine days they would be outdoors during arithmetic lessons working with foot rules and measuring chains, the girls drawing from natural objects rather than copying from pictures. He obtained working model engines with carriages and trucks for the children to examine and handle in order to study the use of steam and a model of a clipper sailing over waves to aid geography. He organised recreation on educational lines to counteract bouts of unruly behaviour and these included the formation of a cricket club for the boys in the adjacent field. In 1912 they visited Wardour Castle taking their *Wiltshire Histories* with them to read the account of the siege which the castle had undergone in the Civil War. There were outings to Salisbury and Old Sarum in Mr Williamson's new motorised van with visits to the museum and other places of interest in order to stimulate their compositions. New life appears to have been breathed into the school to the extent that he could record in November 1913; 'the children were all remarkably punctual this afternoon at 1.15, especially the boys who were simply tumbling over one another in their anxiety to be in good time.'

Able allies in his attempts to revitalise the school were Ellen Whitcombe the infants' teacher and Priscilla Aldwynckle who was originally drawn to Penfound through their mutual interest in music. Miss Aldwynckle's generosity to the children has been mentioned before but now there was a closer bond. Children from the Chase who were unable to get home at dinner time were allowed to eat their lunch on her lawn and she provided soup for seven of the poorer children twice a week. Largely through their efforts money was raised for a school piano and in 1914 they took seventeen of the children to the Wiltshire Musical Festival in Salisbury where, although forming the youngest and smallest of the choirs, the children acquitted themselves well and the judge congratulated them on a most creditable performance.

During long winter evenings Miss Aldwynckle organised meetings of the Band of Mercy for children over seven, its objective being to encourage them to be gentle and considerate to animals. They were taught recitations and songs, and composed stories on paper provided by Mr Penfound. Once a year there was a special evening arranged to entertain their parents:

> . . . Thirty children were present and judging by the excitement and delight shewn by them they enjoyed themselves very much. Eight adult friends kindly assisted with the juveniles during the evening. A Song (Bury a broom) was very nicely rendered by Miss Aldwynckle and five of the girls dressed in character. Mr Penfound was Father Christmas and in an appropriate little speech welcomed everyone to the gathering. The presents comprised useful articles of winter clothing and toys given by Miss Aldwynckle, while many of the garments had been made by Miss Wilson and Miss Cowley of Brookside, Mead End expressly for the Tree. The kind donors were heartily thanked by the children for their gifts and the festivities concluded with the singing of God Save the King. Miss Aldwynckle awarded two school prizes to Evelyn Penn, for good attendance and needlework.
>
> *Parish Papers* 7 January 1914

Mrs Greta Case remembers these events very well and still treasures the book she received on one occasion:

> *Miss Aldwynckle gave me a book for the best essay. We went to the Band of Mercy meetings and she would read to us something and we had to write about it and take it along next month. I never read this book as a child because my parents would not allow it. They thought we were wasting time and gave us a job to do; they were very strict. In the Band of Mercy we were given a card to say we belonged to it and were to carry it with us. If we saw anyone ill-treating an animal we were supposed to go up and show our card!*

The weekly meetings were held at Miss Aldwynckle's on Wednesdays following the end of school. On Thursdays at the same time would be a sewing group preparing garments for the Waifs and Strays, for soldiers during the Great War and even for Belgian refugees housed at Sixpenny Handley in 1915.

It was during this period that Collett re-introduced a competition he had tried many years previously but with little success; that of producing the most attractive Easter egg. Symbolic of the Resurrection, it appears to have been a custom associated with his early life with its strong Russian influence and with Mr Penfound's support it became a regular fixture in the yearly calendar. The egg had to be dyed, not painted, and to achieve this the egg was placed on a piece of damp linen, covered with small pieces of any coloured material and sprinkled with a pinch of dry paint here and there. It would then be tied up carefully and boiled for at least one hour. The eggs were brought to school and numbered to ensure anonymity. Each year a different member of the village community or a visitor would be invited to choose the prettiest eggs. Small money prizes of half a crown downwards were given for the best seven with a penny consolation prize for the rest.

A night school was also started by the new head teacher in 1909 for the benefit of the 'lads and young men' of the parish. It was held from 6.30 to 8.30 p.m. during the winter season on Tuesdays, Thursdays and Saturdays at a fee of 2*d*. a week. It started with a very good attendance of thirty youths and was visited by Mr Bond, Assistant Inspector for the district in the following year who expressed himself pleased with the progress being made although lack of any further references would indicate that interest waned fairly quickly.

Sickness remained a scourge in the village with the Sanitary Inspector and Medical Officer paying regular visits to the school. Scabies, impetigo, ringworm and scarlet fever all supplemented the usual childhood infections in reducing the average attendance. Illegal child employment was also still a source of complaint, both on the agricultural and domestic scene. In May 1913, for example, Penfound wrote in the Log:

> Attendance Officer interviewed Mildred Munday's father. Her age is 12 and she is holding the responsible position of housekeeper – unpaid – to her father (for the last month). Poor Mildred!

During winter months the hours of attendance were re-adjusted to allow the Chase children to arrive home before dark but little allowance was made even for the youngest if they were missing at 9 o'clock in the morning:

> January 6th 11 infants present. Florence and James Munday who live two miles away came this morning just after registers had closed. They, of course, lost their attendance mark.
>
> School Log 1915

Kate Gulliver, who had travelled down from the Chase as a very small infant, remembers Mr Penfound waiting for them at the bottom of

Marleycombe Hill with his stick in his hand. Nor was it always the schoolmaster who complained:

> Sir, why can some keep thear girls from school that is not old enough to leave more than others as others would be glad with thear girls as well as Mrs – time thease things was seen into it is not right if one can do it why not others if not seen into shall write to the headquarters about it from a Villager.

This anonymous and illiterate letter to the schoolmaster in September 1912 may well have come from a prejudiced source but it is clear that Thomas Penfound was not popular in the village. Despite his enlightened methods – or perhaps because of an approach which was considered unorthodox to an essentially conservative rural community – he is remembered by old scholars more for his omissions than his achievements. In 1915 new war directives insisted that the school should be run by a mistress. This led to his marrying Priscilla Aldwynckle by special licence and making an abrupt departure for Newbury leaving Ellen Witcombe, the infants' teacher in temporary charge. In the Log Book he wrote, 'June 18th. I resigned charge of the school today', to which the school correspondent, Mr R.W. Williamson, added in black ink, 'Thank God'!

Mrs Vincent and family, 1885

Mrs Hardwick took over just at the time Bowerchalke was beginning to realise there was a war on! A teacher of long experience, she had followed her husband down from Bristol to Salisbury where he was engaged in a military capacity. A measles epidemic lengthened the Harvest Holiday that year giving plenty of time for a promised renovation, so that the school was newly colour-washed and cleaned on her arrival. Although the slow round of rural life continued very much as it always had, news of terrible happenings began to trickle in from relatives at the front and labour was becoming very scarce. Boys were granted permission to leave school early because of the shortage on the land and the headmistress herself was granted a day's leave in January 1916 to see her son off to France. Permission was also granted to the children to have afternoons off in order to pick blackberries for jam for the troops, a chore they eagerly agreed to, picking well over 200 lbs in a single afternoon on one occasion.

Mrs Hardwick wished to be nearer her husband ten miles away in Salisbury so she resigned after two years. She had enjoyed her time at Bowerchalke and was later to return to the village for a long and fruitful period. Ellen Witcombe, the assistant teacher who, for nearly fourteen years had worked so devotedly with overcrowded infant classes was removed by the Wiltshire Education Department because the numbers had fallen. Mrs Bessie Wilson, therefore, who was appointed in October 1917, must have known that her task was not an easy one – especially as the fall in numbers appears to have been a fairly temporary affair. Within a very short time the Inspector was again complaining at the overcrowded conditions, thirty infants being squashed into a room meant for twenty-four.

Working with cheerful resignation Mrs Wilson completed the period under review. The tedious outbreaks of sickness were still recorded: bad teeth, boils and impetigo all pointing, perhaps, to dietary deficiencies. In July 1918, for example, is recorded 'several of the children have breakings out. Attendance Officer called for Medical Officer for soap and water.' Two children were found to be suffering from fits and there were several cases of mental deficiency. The presence in the village of a School Nurse by this time must have been very reassuring to Mrs Wilson.

Apart from blackberry picking, the children did their part in the war effort by going round the parish with little red flags to sell at a penny each in aid of Red Cross funds and parcels for the prisoners of war. Money was raised by their concerts such as this successful presentation of 'Dame Durden's Shoe':

> The Children's Musical Play was performed on Monday last with unquestionable success and was appreciated by a crowded audience. The perfect manner in which the children had been taught their parts was simply marvellous and reflected great credit upon Mrs Hardwick. Even the infants did everything

well . . . Miss Nellie Goodfellow very kindly played all the accompaniments.
Parish Papers 26 April 1916

Miss Nellie Goodfellow had also taken over Miss Aldwynckle's after-school sewing group employing the girls in knitting comforts for the troops. The modest efforts of this small school are recorded by Collett over a two-year period:

	£	*s.*	*d.*
Concerts given in the school	6	4	10
By sale of flags (2 years)	6	13	0
Collections on two Empire Days (Comforts for the Troops)	2	6	6
Jack Cornwell Memorial		10	0
Christmas Day collection for destitute Belgians	2	18	0
Total	18	12	4

In November 1919, with the war long over, Mrs Wilson received permission for the school to be closed in order to meet her husband, a Regimental Sergeant Major, arriving home from Mesopotamia after an absence of three and a half years. With one era finally ending another was beginning. The County Council appointed a specialist Domestic Science teacher to tour the villages giving instruction, for a month at a time, in cooking and other household work. As the school was not large enough for this purpose, the girls were sent to Broadchalke School. Thus came the first impetus in a trend which many years later would take education out of the village altogether.

THE HOLIDAY CHILDREN

However controversial, ritualistic or just plain dogmatic Edward Collett may have appeared to the adult world, his affection and concern for children were beyond question. Harold (Teddy) Trowbridge, who was born at Woodminton in 1903, sums up the feelings many have expressed:

Edward Collett was a very kindly man. He was quite tall and rather Russian-looking with a great sense of humour. He always had children trailing after him because he was such great fun.

His interest in the welfare of young people, however, extended far beyond that of home, church and school. In the *Parish Paper* of 6 August 1903 he reported:

> Last Monday by kind permission of Rev Margesson we had a pleasant little visit from a party of 8 merry London boys who have been holiday making at Ebbsborne. Some of them are choristers at All Hallows Poplar. Mrs Bracher was good enough to lend them her field for games and they also had a ramble on the down. A picnic Tea was provided for them on the Vicarage lawn after which came races and games which were heartily joined in. Mr Linnell and Mr Arthur Owen (a visitor) helped greatly in entertaining the boys.

This is the first reference of any connection with London children and may have been his introduction to the Church of the Holy Trinity, Greenwich, for in 1905 parties of children from that parish began to arrive at fortnightly intervals during the summer to stay in the homes of welcoming cottagers. Supported by the Children's Country Holiday Fund, families in Greenwich were enabled, through their local schools, to pay small weekly amounts for the opportunity of getting their children away from the smoky atmosphere of the city into the tranquility of the countryside. To help them with this project Collett had persuaded certain of the cottagers, for a very modest payment, to make room in their already overcrowded accommodation for one or two more. Collett's remarks on the arrival of the first group, however, were hardly calculated to please their hosts!

> Our holiday children have arrived and bonny little things they are: 10 girls and 6 boys fresh from London with all the beautiful sharpness of the cultivated life of the town. It is such a treat to see brilliant examples of 'life' after our dull little folks here delightful as they are in their quiet way.
>
> *Parish Papers* 29 July 1905

The village took great pleasure in entertaining their visitors, and the London treasurer remarked in a letter to Collett that nowhere had they received a more kindly welcome, or been more carefully looked after.

The following year was marred by the unfortunate death of Ellen Meads. Arriving as one of the first party of children at Salisbury Station in beautiful summer weather, Ellen had felt sick and faint in the train. She was carefully put in the waggon and brought back to the carrier's wife, Mrs Williams, who was to be her hostess. There she died the following morning, her mother having been telegraphed to come at once. The funeral must have been impressive, the coffin was carried by the six London boys and followed by the nine other visiting girls, Ellen's parents and a large number of the villagers. Such moments can unite unlikely forces so that Collett commented, 'We were especially touched by the generous and sympathetic offerings of the Dissenters, who entirely of their own free will made gifts of money and assistance of various kinds.'

Further evidence of the kindness and goodwill engendered on these occasions – not just in Bowerchalke but in other country areas as well – is amusingly illustrated in the magazine of Holy Trinity Church, Greenwich in October 1907 where the vicar commented:

> It is a great pleasure to find that our children are treated so well by our country friends, especially as the remuneration is small and there can be little financial gain accruing to them from the children's stay. If anyone wishes to be convinced of this let him meet a returning party of our children at one of the railway terminii, and note the number of parcels, bags, boxes, etc., some containing live fowls, rabbits and ducks and affording often a perplexing problem to the visitor who has to convey the children across London to their homes.

Other successful holidays were enjoyed in subsequent years, each fortnight concluding with tea on the vicarage lawn and games organised by John Linnell in a meadow opposite which was loaned for the occasion by the Foyle family. In 1910 sickness in the village prevented the holidays taking place. During the First World War they stopped altogether and although groups were accommodated in 1920, it would seem that Collett's failing health and the difficulty in getting suitable homes prevented them coming again.

The Waifs and Strays

Collett's concern for the needs of underprivileged children was displayed much more permanently through his almost lifelong support of the Waifs and Strays Society. For years he had raised funds in the village, especially for their Boys' Home at Islington, but for more practical help we must return to Jane Wilkins who had followed her mother as mistress of the remote Chase School. In 1898 Collett had been urging villagers to consider opening a home for unwanted children and had received promises of help with subscriptions for coal and extra lights during the winter months should such a home commence. At the beginning of 1890 the Revd J.G. Munro, from the Waifs and Strays Society, visited a fund-raising concert and had spoken of its work emphasising the great need that existed. Miss Wilkins was sufficiently impressed by this talk to consider such a venture. In July, Collett, urging the children of the parish to purchase the quarterly magazine, *Our Brothers and Sisters* and assist their work stated:

> We should like to start a branch here that our own children might take part. It is natural that our interest in this matter should be quickened by the fact that we have now got a little fatherless boy living in the parish whose case was

taken up by the Society and under whose rules he is being taken care of by Miss Wilkins. We hope very soon to have another child put into our keeping from the same source.

Parish Papers 3 July 1890

Jane Wilkins resigned her position at the Chase School at the end of that term to open the small cottage home in Quidham Street she shared with her son, Stanley, for this work. By October Willie Thomson, the first arrival, had been joined by two others and the village had obviously taken them to their hearts. Soup was sent regularly by Mrs Butler from Rookhaye, presents of toys and illustrated magazines came from others and the local doctor had promised his services free. By 1893 the number of children had risen to six and Collett was able to report proudly that, according to the rules of the Society, the cottage was now to be recognised, rather grandly for such a small establishment, as St Bartholomew's Home.

It was visited regularly by the Society's woman doctor to ensure all was well and Miss Wilkins' care was always complimented. By 1897, however, some of the original group had already left the home, their places being taken by others. The eldest of this first group, Raymond Newman, had arrived at the age of eight just after his father's death, his mother having been left with a large family was unable to cope. Having now reached the age limit of fourteen Raymond became apprenticed as a printer at the *Salisbury Times* office. William Bishop Pearce, another boy from the home, went to a grocer's shop in the same city. Charles Hugh Devereaux needed special medical treatment and was transferred to a larger home in Lincoln. After twelve years of this work Miss Wilkins was taken seriously ill and died shortly after in 1903. The home was broken up but Mrs Eliza Williams, sister-in-law of the village carrier, took the remaining children into her tiny cottage in Church Street. She was very fond of children and was spoken of warmly for her care by the village as well as by the Society's lady doctor on her periodic visits.

Collett took a close interest in the welfare of these underprivileged children. They played a prominent part in his growing choir and many are remembered as helping in the vicarage – cheap labour perhaps but, as the vicar appears to have given away a large portion of his meagre income in one form or another, his motives are more likely to have been based on pastoral concern. Certainly, many of them continued to correspond with him for years after they had left the village. Hugh Devereaux, for example, went to Canada at the expense of the Society. A picture of him appeared in the Society's magazine in September 1902 as 'one of our successful emigrants'. He was taught leathercraft and enlisted as a saddler in the Canadian Dragoons where he was promoted to corporal. Another in British Columbia, Walter McTier, was still corresponding in 1920 when he wrote:

BOWERCHALKE

WEEKLY PARISH PAPER.

"THAT YE MIGHT KNOW OUR AFFAIRS" EPH. VI. 22.

No. 1491.] WEDNESDAY, DECEMBER 12, 1917. [PRICE ½d.

TOMORROW EVENING, AT HALF-PAST-SIX,
THERE WILL BE AN ADVENT SERVICE, WITH SERMON BY THE
REV. ERNEST E. HASLUCK,
Vicar of S. Mary's, Handley.

THIS AND THAT.

THE MOON.—New Moon, next Friday, Dec. 14, at 9·17 A.M.

LIGHTING-UP-TIME.—Today : 4·19 Next Wednesday : 4·20.

SERMON TEXTS—Last Thursday (by the Rev. Wm. D. Hawken : "GOD commandeth all men everywhere to repent." Acts 17, 30 On Sunday last : *M.* "The way of the LORD is an undefiled way." Ps. 18, 30. *E.* "We know that the SON OF GOD is come." 1 S. Jn 5, 20.

NEXT SUNDAY.—*3rd. Sunday in Advent,* December 16. Church-colour : *Violet.* HYMNS. At Mattins : Pro 46, 49, 420, 379, Rec.48. At Evensong : (Mission Hymns). Pro 21, 42, 72, 102, Rec.124.

HOLY DAY.—[See Prayer-Book Calendar.] Tomorrow (Dec. 13) S. Lucy, Virgin and Martyr, A.D 304.

OUR PARISH NURSE—(for Broadchalke and Bowerchalke) has come into residence, and begun her good work amongst us. It has been decided by the Committee, that she should live in Bowerchalke, and she is lodging at Mrs. Goodfellow's. Her name is Miss Smithers, and she comes from the Wilts Nursing Association. We offer her a very hearty welcome, and shall greatly appreciate her skilled help in ministering to all those who may be in sickness or suffering.

CHRISTMAS CONCERT.—The School Children are busily preparing for the Entertainment which Mrs. Wilson is arranging for them to give during Christmas week. It will probably take place on the Wednesday and Thursday, Dec. 26, and 27. Next week we shall hope to give full particulars, and name of the piece they will act. Tickets will be ready beforehand, for which numbered Chairs will be kept.

ON SATURDAY AFTERNOONS—a happy little company of Children meet together in the Class-room of the School, under the direction of Miss Nellie Goodfellow, to make little garments, and to make little picture-books, for the poor Orphan Infants of the many brave Soldiers who have fallen in the War. This work is undertaken at the suggestion of the Waifs & Strays Society, whose CHRIST-like care of the sad and homeless, must move every human being to sweet compassion.

THE MONTHLY MAGAZINE.—The following notice appears in this month's number : Owing to the increased cost of labour and material it has been decided to raise the price in 1918 to 1½*d.* Will any subscribers who wish to leave off taking the Magazine, give notice to that effect, not later than Saturday next, December 15.

NOTICE.—THE BUS.—On Christmas Eve (Monday-week) the Bus will run to Salisbury at 5·30 P.M, as on Saturdays.

LOST—A Brown Woollen GLOVE (left-hand).
For the name of the owner, please apply at the Vicarage.

Printed at the Vicarage Private Printing Press, Bowerchalke.

Parish Papers Wednesday 12 December 1917

> I thank you for still sending me the Parish Paper. It is so very pleasant to know you still have me in remembrance after so many years absence from dear old Bowerchalke. I have great hopes of being able to visit you all again. Meanwhile the Paper is always very welcome and I enjoy reading it immensely. . . .
>
> *Parish Papers* 12 May 1920

William Bishop Pearce served with the 2nd Wilts Regiment during the Boer War. On his return from South Africa in 1903 he received a hero's welcome in the village, taking his place once more in the choir and joining the Club Dinner before rejoining his regiment at Aldershot. Later in his career, a bout of enteric fever shattered his strong constitution and he was invalided out of the services in 1910 to die shortly after of consumption.

A fuller picture emerges of the subsequent career of Raymond Newman. During his five and a half years' apprenticeship at the *Salisbury Times* he was never late or absent from his work once – an example the vicar was quick to hold up to the rest of the village – and as a result was presented with a token of their appreciation by his employers. After a further two years he obtained a position in London, but while travelling on holiday in 1913 he was involved in a railway accident at Yeovil. He was sitting in the end carriage of the excursion train when another engine struck it. He was hurled with such violence against the opposite side of the carriage that his head was forced through the woodwork and his legs, fixed between the broken seats, were so badly crushed that one had to be amputated immediately. Such was his spirit that he made remarkable progress from his injuries and appears to have returned to work fairly quickly.

Claud Aldin's story is sadder. Having been deserted in 1903 by both his parents in Accrington at the age of six, Claud came to live with Mrs Williams. He was a popular boy at school where he gained prizes for his good attendance and collected the offertory during the services. Never a strong boy, he developed lung disease and, shortly after going to work at the schoolhouse in Wilton, died of consumption. The children had an afternoon off school to attend his funeral and a memorial cross to mark his grave was funded by the village.

Mrs Eliza Williams had little good fortune with her own children, all but one being stillborn, but her devotion to the Waifs and Strays over a great number of years is clear. In 1914, however, Mabel Hardy was recorded as the last remaining child to be medically examined. After that there is no further reference although the village continued to support the Society's work through its branch of the Children's Union, sales of work and a Saturday morning sewing party to produce toys which Nellie Goodfellow, a Sunday school teacher, continued to run for many years.

6
Entertainment

> We no longer get a garden show, there is no cricket club, our enjoyable humorous entertainments of former years have faded away and now if the Club Fete dies out also we shall think that Bowerchalke is one of the dullest places in the County of Wiltshire.
>
> *Parish Papers* 6 May 1914

Collett's lament at the fading cultural life of Bowerchalke may have been as much regret at his own diminishing vigour as the waning of village activity. Nevertheless, there is no doubt that the new insurance legislation with its effects on the Friendly Society, the outbreak of the First World War and the development of rural transport all served to alter the social life of an area still comparatively isolated from the 'fleshpots' of Salisbury. Collett's involvement in social activities outside his church had been largely that of innovator and encourager rather than participator, but he helped enliven the drab lives of the cottagers by badgering the reluctant tenant farmers into action or by persuading them to dig deeper into their pockets for annual subscriptions. As an interested bystander, he was then able to record ensuing events in his paper.

Early efforts on Collett's part to establish an annual Flower Show had met with resounding apathy so that by 1882, when May storms wreaked havoc with the sprouting plants and did 'great hurt to all the stone fruit trees', it was called off for that year with scathing comment in the *Parish Paper*. No mention of further efforts was made until four years later when a Potato Show was held in the schoolroom:

> The potato being as everybody will admit, the *most* important vegetable grown, and the most useful, it is very desirable that every means should be used to improve its cultivation. An Exhibition such as the one we contemplate, solely devoted to the interest of this plant, and endeavouring to set forth every feature connected with its growth, ought to be of considerable usefulness. . . .
>
> *Parish Papers* 5 August 1886

An event devoted entirely to the display of potatoes might seem a trifle dull today but the occasion proved surprisingly successful with Lord Pembroke and the local MP, Sir Thomas Grove, contributing towards the prize money and the Bishop of Salisbury's head gardener acting as judge. Suttons, the famous seed growers from Reading, and the nurseries at Hilperton both agreed to set up exhibitions of their best strains of seed stock and the villagers proudly displayed their 'rounds' and 'kidneys' of various classes to compete for the prizes. Nor were the women forgotten. They had been warned well in advance to start practising for the best dishes of eight boiled potatoes, (both peeled and unpeeled), and there were other sections for potatoes boiled, fried, mashed or cooked in thin slices. A potato-peeling competition, however, for the quickest work with the thinnest parings did not appeal to the timid housewives of Bowerchalke and was called off.

Perhaps because of this successful venture, renewed attempts were made to establish a Flower Show in the interests of the working men of the village. Early in 1888 a committee with Collett as chairman, Mr Caddy the schoolmaster as secretary, and including six cottagers was established, but at the public meeting called for June their efforts again foundered on the indifference of those who should have provided leadership:

> A Meeting of the Committee was held in the Schoolroom on Monday evening last, at which the greater part of the farmers and tradespeople of the parish shewed their interest by their absence. If a Flower Show is really a benefit to the place and people, ought it not to receive the personal interest and sympathy of those who are the employers of labour or who are otherwise in a position of responsibility? But it seems here to be the rule for the 'big people' to take no interest in anything that involves trouble or expense, until the 'little people' have overcome them both. This strikes one as being rather odd.
>
> *Parish Papers* 21 June 1888

This seems to have shamed them into activity for the resulting show on Wednesday 31 July was undoubtedly a resounding success and set the tone for many years to come.

The village was astir very early, despite the poor weather in order to prepare the field. Nervous committee members decorated Shrewsbury Harding's barn in Quidham Street with flags, banners, evergreens, flowers and large numbers of hothouse plants, the tables neatly arranged and covered with paper or linen so that exhibits could be placed with skill and care. By 11.30 a.m. over two hundred exhibits were in position to be judged by Mr F. Smith, the Bishop's head gardener and his helpers despite a poor growing season, and it was getting on for the official opening by the time they had finished. During the lunch hour, the Bowerchalke Brass Band, led by John Linnell, was driven in Williamson's farm waggon through the neighbouring village of Broadchalke as a reminder of the big event before returning to parade through Bowerchalke. By 4 o'clock a large crowd had assembled for the public tea arranged by Ellen Coombs and her committee of ladies. W.H. Gramshaw, the South Wilts Conservative candidate, had ridden over between other engagements to preside and was joined by other dignatories from the surrounding area.

After the tea villagers moved to the adjoining field to listen to the band and cheer on the sports, with Mr Gramshaw joining in the spirit of the occasion by acting as starter. Dancing, Aunt Sally, Coconut shying and other activities continued until dark when everyone returned to their homes well satisfied that the day had been by far the most pleasant and best-managed that the little village had seen.

An even better event was held in 1889 when the title was changed from Flower to Garden Show, an acknowledgement of the full range of exhibits which were much improved that year in quality and quantity. The gaiety of the displays, this time housed in Williamson's huge cart shed, was further enhanced by generous offerings of dahlias and hothouse plants sent for display rather than competition by wealthier well-wishers, a simpler note being added by nosegays of wild flowers arranged by the schoolchildren. On other occasions donkey and wheelbarrow races are recorded, walking races for the over forty-fives, eight-a-side tug-of-war between rival farms and the glaring lamps of Weldon's Pleasure Booth giving the impression in the distant gloom, as Collett observed, 'as though they were living in a busy

The Foyle family, 5 October 1887. As wheelwrights, the Foyles were central to the village economy

town'. Events did not always proceed smoothly. In 1892, for example, a great deal of fruit was stolen from the display plates, an event which led Collett to observe wryly that if the greedy rogues had been content with the onions it would have been much easier to follow them up. In subsequent years, the stern presence of Police Sergeant Goddard was abroad to prevent a recurrence.

By the beginning of the new century attempts were being made to provide fresh novelties for the Garden Show, a need well met for a while by the proprietors of the Sunlight Soap Company who in 1900 provided a Monkey Soap Prize Competition for whoever could shine the most pennies. Entrants were confined to women with the prizes displayed beforehand in John Dimmer's shop: 12 electro-plated teaspoons and a pair of sugar tongs (value one guinea) for the winner with several additional boxes of soap for runners-up. The next year Sunlight organised a Washing Competition. A towel, a bucket of water, a piece of Sunlight soap, a chair and two clothes pegs were provided and at 6.30 p.m. each of twelve contestants up to her elbows in froth and bubbles, scrubbed furiously at her towel loudly cheered on by family and friends. There were three prizes for the cleanest results and the unlucky losers were allowed to keep their towels as consolation prizes.

Like any other village at that time or this, the necessity to raise funds for worthy causes provided a major channel for social gatherings. The bazaars and jumble sales in aid of the church fabric, the Waifs and Strays or – following the War – the Nursing Fund, new Village Hall and the Soldiers' Memorial, all created such opportunities in a less sophisticated era for village get-togethers with the more genteel ladies displaying their social graces and organising ability. The Industrial Exhibitions in 1880 and 1889, for example, linked with a Sale of Work brought together arts and crafts made by the villagers themselves with other items of local interest loaned for the occasion, although few details are given. The Exhibition of 1903, however, gives a clearer glimpse into the Victorian home of at least the better-off, the tiny schoolroom cluttered with pictures, china, needlework, rare prints and books, stuffed birds, mechanical toys, fretwork, wood carving, historical relics and Victorian curios of all kinds. The cottagers, I suspect, would have had far less to show although everyone was urged to exhibit something however humble. The Scrap Sale or 'Sale of Work' was more overtly geared to the needs of the labourer's wives with their large families to clothe:

> . . . We venture to suggest that the articles should very nearly all be useful rather than ornamental, so as to suit the actual requirements of working people. We do not aim at a *fancy* sale but we should like to combine real usefulness to our purchasers with the gain which will aid the fund we have to

raise. With this intention our richer friends can help us very materially by contributing any garments they have no further use for or which their children have outgrown.

Parish Papers 9 May 1889

'Our Parish Pastime took place last Tuesday, and was very successful and enjoyable. There was no formal programme so that the entertainment was like a family party.' Thus Collett describes the social event that more than any other drew the various elements of village life together through an avenue of mutual enjoyment. Often performed to packed audiences in the ill-ventilated schoolroom, 'the entertainment' was the means whereby the village, with the help of friends and the occasional more distinguished artist, could 'put on a show'.

The *Parish Papers* are full of references to these events: advance notices, details of the programme, reviews, but never a plea for volunteers for these were always forthcoming. One man, for instance, walked all the way from Ebbesbourne Wake one evening in torrential rain for the sheer enjoyment of singing. Collett's account of the concert in January 1885 gives a clear idea of the practical problems that were involved:

THE ENTERTAINMENT, of which we gave notice in our last, came off most successfully last night (Thurs). Mrs Coombs, with her accustomed zeal and unflagging perseverance and ably assisted in all her efforts by her sister Miss Fanny Stone, and others, had been working hard for some weeks past to produce the good results we had the pleasure to participate in yesterday. The whole of the day was taken up in getting the room ready, it was comfortably arranged and well lighted. A temporary platform was cleverly erected under the superintendence of Mr Coombs. The piano was kindly lent by Miss Stone. There was a large and appreciative attendance and an entire absence of 'rowdyism' in the back rows, which was very satisfactory. Sgt Webb was on duty outside, and effectually prevented some idle loungers from hanging about the School yard and listening at the windows, and so – with characteristic meanness – getting, for nothing, an entertainment which was worth paying for. . . .

Parish Papers 30 January 1885

The vicar's modest contribution on this occasion was not named, but the programme, to raise funds for the Chase School, was full of popular Victorian melodies calculated to stir the emotions, the headmistress, Jane Wilkins, playing a prominent part:

Part I

Pianoforte Duet:	Echo of Lucerne	Misses Stone and Major
Solo and chorus:	God bless the Prince of Wales	

Song:	When the thorn is white Miss Stone
Song:	Strike the iron while it's hot Mr Andrews
Song:	Auntie Miss Kingsbury
Reading:	Rev T.N. Hutchinson
Pianoforte Solo:	Grand March Miss Roper
Song:	Fading away Mrs Coombs
Glee:	Let the hills resound
Song:	Round goes the wheel Mr H. Hitchings
Duet:	List to the Convent Bells Misses Wilkins and A Stone
Song:	Never mind the rest

Part II

Instrumental Piece:	Mr and Mrs Elliott
Song:	The broken pitcher Miss Kingsbury
Song:	Doctor Quack Mr H. Hitchings
Song:	Silver threads among the gold Miss Wilkins
Song:	Mr C. Elliott
Reading:	Rev E. Collett
Pianoforte Solo:	Miss Kingsbury
Trio:	The Mermaids song Misses Major, Elliott and Wilkins
Song:	Three Jolly Britons Mr Andrews
Song:	Next May Day Miss Elliott
Song:	I can beat him at that Miss Stone
Glee:	Sleep while soft evening breezes blow

GOD SAVE THE QUEEN

J.M. Hayden, a Professor of Music and lay vicar at Salisbury Cathedral, performed piano solos on more than one occasion; Winnie Warren, a distinguished violinist and medallist from the Royal College of Music was another welcome guest accompanied by her husband playing the piano. On a memorable evening in December 1915 a concert was given by the choir of King's College, Cambridge, whose association with Bowerchalke through its church remains today. More popular one suspects, were Mr and Mrs Dinah, original Pierrots (clowns), or the Grahames ('late of the Lyceum, Standard and Royal Theatres'), with their celebrated programme of comic songs, conjuring tricks and humorous sketches. Ventriloquism, too, was always very popular if done well, as by Professor Du Cann on another memorable occasion in 1888, (despite having been mistakenly booked for a Friday – 'that being the weekly commemoration of Our Lord's Death and therefore not a suitable day for occasions of merriment'):

Professor Du Cann's entertainment last week proved itself very full of interest and fun. The ventriloquism was decidedly the best part of the performance and was exceedingly good. We were *quite* taken in, for a few minutes by the voice outside the window! The old woman under the chair and the other who tried to get in at the class room door were admirably done. And so were little 'Miss Wilkins' in the bag and the speaking head.

Parish Papers 3 May 1888

One of the most popular and frequent visitors was George Foote, a pedlar, actor and itinerant entertainer. In his 'Merry Hour' for the children, he used his comic antics for the more sombre purpose of driving home important moral lessons, but his evening performances of 'Foote's Funny Fancies' included songs, comic sketches and brilliant imitations of musical instruments performed with grotesque humorous contortions of the face that reputedly had his audience writhing in their seats. On one occasion he kept the full attention of a packed house for nearly two hours with amusing recollections of his life as an actor over forty years, but like many a clown his private life was lonely and he died at Portland in 1922 unknown and undernourished.

Among the village entertainers John Linnell played an increasingly prominent part as he grew from gawky adolescence into the 'flash dog' that

Bernard Harrington in traditional smock, 1885

he later became, with his finger in just about every village pie. As a singer and organiser he was much involved in most productions, the proceeds of the Easter Concert coming back to him each year for his services as the church organist. The Elliott family from Woodminton, parents and daughters, usually took a prominent part, sometimes organising a complete entertainment on their own. With the coming of the schoolmaster, Thomas Penfound, a popular Glee Club was founded to augment the choruses and his discreet romance with Priscilla Aldwynckle blossomed through their joint musical interests. It was the humorous sketches that usually stole the evening. Light and inconsequential, they gave the villagers a chance to laugh at themselves and for labourers to forget their dull cottages and long hours of toil. It would be interesting to see what impression 'Grumpy's Blunder' or 'Mrs Mulligatawny's Spring Cleaning' would make on today's audiences, reared on the professionalism of British television.

In September 1900 came the first mention of a modern dance in Bowerchalke. It was organised by the Williamson family when they opened up their grounds at Knowle Farm to celebrate Harvest Home. It was obviously successful for on Boxing Night it was repeated and then became an annual fixture. Gradually through the decade the dance and social became an increasingly popular addition to the Bowerchalke calendar, particularly amongst the young, either at Knowle Farm or in the schoolroom with Miss Aldwynckle presiding at the piano.

Another popular diversion on winter evenings was the Magic Lantern. The village does not appear to have owned one of its own for when the vicar's brother John was appointed to the living of Teffont, Frank Golden, a village lad in his service, cycled over with their machine, a precarious journey with such a load across the steep downland of Fovant Hollow. Used extensively by the Society for the Propagation of the Gospel to illustrate its missionary work in many fields the Magic Lantern was also used to good effect in the village for colonial recruitment or for other charities such as the Waifs and Strays. As pure entertainment it was also a popular adjunct to the Sunday and Day school winter treats although the darkened room was a fruitful opportunity for unwelcome high spirits:

> A MAGIC LANTERN was exhibited, in the school room, last night, by a Mr Davidson. The views were principally taken from scenes in the more recent wars in which Gt Britain has been engaged. There were a few comic slides at the end. What *might* perhaps have been enjoyable was completely spoiled by the unmeaning noises and utterances of some ill mannered persons, who greeted the appearance of almost every picture with merriment, no matter how sober the subject!
>
> *Parish Papers* 16 October 1885

The Church Army van which appeared for the first time in 1899 was popular for its novelty as much as its religious significance but could also use the lantern to good effect. A substantial-looking vehicle painted dark green and bearing texts in white letters which gave it, according to Collett, an ugly and rather 'shoppy' appearance, it was towed from one village to another by a pair of strong farm horses loaned by the receiving village. Stationed in Bracher's meadow, it was the centre for evangelical open-air meetings followed by an address with Magic Lantern pictures to packed audiences in the schoolroom or the church.

In 1901 the first moving pictures appeared, although in those early days the programme was shown in conjunction with other entertainment. On this occasion Mr R.G. Law (also known as Professor Vaux) showed pictures of battles and stirring incidents in the Boer War interspersed with his own demonstration of conjuring and ventriloquism. By 1907 Pool and Laws' improved 2,000 candle-power Bioscope was being used to show 'breathtaking' scenes such as Alpine climbing in polar regions or 'the phantom ride on an express train through the famous Peaks of Derbyshire.' Comedy remained king, however, and 'The Washerwoman and the Sweep' showed how humour could be depicted on the screen in a way impossible on the stage ('Sweep kisses the laundrymaid – he is very black – requires washing – they do it – must be mangled – it is done – very flat – hung on the clothes line to dry'). By 1908 a visit from the Cinematograph Company had become an eagerly-awaited event:

> THE ENTERTAINMENTS given in the schoolroom on Monday and Tuesday by Mr Harry Newman's Picture and Concert Party were excellent and most enjoyable. The attendance was so large that many were unable to obtain admission. All the arrangements were undertaken by the performers themselves who provided their own platform and also the sheet for exhibiting the Moving Pictures. The first part consisted of songs, ventriloquism and conjuring all of which were done singularly well and to great enjoyment. Then after a very short interval we were treated to some splendid moving pictures many of which were irresistibly laughable.
>
> *Parish Papers* 5 November 1908

The gramophone, too, was a highly prized novelty at the beginning of the century possessed by only a few. Bill Gatehouse at Castle appears to have owned the only one in Bowerchalke but the village was able to share his enjoyment. In 1905 he gave a recital of his records to a crowded schoolroom all curious to enjoy this new experience. The records were described as good and clear and the event was used as an excuse to hear once more the duologue and comic sketch from the previous week's entertainment. After two more years the improved 'phonograph' was bringing even more clarity to the sound:

THE PHONOGRAPH which the Rev F. Raikes was so good as to bring over for our pleasure on Thursday last was very highly appreciated by all who had the privilege of hearing it. It certainly is a beautiful piece of mechanism and reproduces the human voice and every kind of sound with marvellous precision and clearness. Some of the selections were humorous, others sentimental and a few were quite dramatic (as for instance the weird story of the ghost). There was a complete absence of the metallic tone so prevalent in many of the inferior class of instruments. The children had their own (free) entertainment at 5.30 and at 7 o'clock the adults had their turn at the small charge of 1*d*.

Parish Papers 21 November 1907

Gradually, the gramophone came into fairly common use and until the village was able to purchase its own piano it was a welcome guest at any party or dance.

Primrose League teas organised by one or another of the more aspiring ladies, farm suppers at Christmas or harvest-time for the labourers, Club holidays, choir dinners, and homespun entertainments of various kinds; Bowerchalke does not appear to have mouldered in its comparative rural isolation. In 1911 Collett even arranged a regular weekly practice of indoor games such as draughts, dominoes, and card games with a view to holding competitions with neighbouring parishes. For the more seriously- inclined there were Penny Readings, simple and informal gatherings in private houses to while away a winter's evening with songs and readings at the cost of a penny's admission. The Wiltshire Arts and Crafts Association existed to 'employ profitably the idle hours of lads and girls and others who suffer from the lack of attractive occupation by providing interests which will keep them happily engaged at home', high-flown objectives for those who had little domestic space or encouragement. However, Nellie Goodfellow and Priscilla Aldwinckle both opened their homes for various skills like needlework, crochet, painting and various forms of woodwork to be enjoyed for practical ends such as the making of dolls and toys for the Salisbury Infirmary.

During the summer months life was lived mainly outside. Gardening, walking on the gentle rolling downland of Marleycombe or just passing the time of day with neighbours were probably the most popular pastimes then. The Bowerchalke Brass Band formed, declined and re-formed again with John Linnell and the Foyle family taking a prominent part, its presence adding colour and gaiety to all village festivities. There are a few sparse references to a Soccer Club but the chief sport was undoubtedly cricket. The first references come in 1900 with Collett, who was obviously no sportsman, rather saddened that the Hindon Choir had travelled so far to play and yet lost the match. Attempts to form a village team on a permanent basis always foundered on the difficulty of obtaining a suitable pitch.

Farm workers taking a rest from the exhausting task of harvesting, 1890

Linnell, to whom cricket represented a lifetime's passion, recalled just before his death at ninety-two, that games had been played on Marleycombe although such a sloping surface must have been highly unsuitable. Foyle, Hardiman, and Williamson all loaned fields for a period but play would have been dependent on agricultural requirements and it was not until 1920 that the Beckley family, who followed the Hardings at Manor Farm, loaned the beautiful tree-lined field that enabled Bowerchalke to develop one of the best village sides in the Salisbury area.

The difficulties of finding suitable cricket pitches led the young men of the village, with their 'irrepressible playing instincts', to look elsewhere for their pleasures and in 1900 they developed a taste for quoits, a skilfull game involving the pitching of horseshoes over a post. A game was organised in the Habgood's orchard against Coombe Bissett which Robert Williamson, the watercress grower, found so enjoyable that he sent a note round the village: 'I have bought a set of 6lb quoits which I shall be pleased to lend to our Bowerchalke men and also find them a place to practise.' A club was duly formed with Williamson as treasurer and Tom Habgood, from the Bell Inn, as secretary. The entrance fee was 6*d.* and a weekly payment of 1*d.* enabled them to join in the games and practice three evenings a week on the new beds put down on Knowle Green. Any surplus funds were put aside and used for a dinner at the end of each season.

Oddly enough the sport that Bowerchalke seemed most to excel in was rifle shooting. Practices were held on Friday evenings during the winter months in the schoolroom under the expert guidance of Captain Cartwright, master of the Wilton Hounds, whose stately residence, 'Upwood', was situated in a no-man's land between Bowerchalke and Handley. Space must have been rather confined but, as Fred Penny recalls, 'we used to put a target in the class room and shoot from just inside the door at the other end.' With an enthusiastic membership of over thirty there was no shortage of match players, Arthur Lush, a shepherd's son, and William Case, a young farmer, being among its most capable representatives. There is no record of them ever losing a match. It was even suggested that in addition to the '3 R's', a fourth should be taught in schools – the rifle.

It would be wrong to conclude this chapter with the impression that life in Bowerchalke was completely centred within itself. For many, it is true, there was little existence outside the immediate vicinity of the adjacent fields and villages or an occasional visit to town on market day. Nevertheless, the carrier's cart, bicycle or even 'Shanks's Pony' would be used to arrive at the site of an event if the attraction was sufficiently strong as on this red letter day when Barnum's internationally-renowned circus arrived:

> BARNUM! It was not surprising that when the notice was given that the 'Greatest Show on earth' was going to visit Salisbury nearly everybody in all the country round should have immediately gone mad with excitement and delight! Thousands of people made a point of going to see it and as far as we know no one was disappointed. We are very glad they had such a good chance of enjoying themselves for it is a healthy recreation to mind and body and a help to a better understanding of the wonders of the great world outside our little village. . . .
>
> *Parish Papers* 13 July 1899

On another occasion in 1903 a Wild West Show in Salisbury proved such an attraction that the dedication of a memorial plaque to Sidney Williams who died serving in India had to be postponed – one could hardly hold this service when his father, the carrier, was busy ferrying people to such a bonanza!

By 1912 when Collett observed that Salisbury Fair that autumn was so much less rowdy an event than that experienced by their forefathers, it was a much quicker and smoother journey in the new Bowerchalke motor bus, but this social revolution was to be interrupted by events of a sadder nature. Together, they were to change the village forever.

7
The First World War

> It has been said that a new England is being born in the trenches of Flanders.
> Bishop of Salisbury 1914

> We have also had a letter from Bertie Coombs, one of our former choir boys. He writes from Salonica. He says he has just received the Parish Paper from home and not only did it come as a pleasant surprise but it also brought many happy memories of the good old school days and old friends many of whom have since given their lives for their country.
> *Parish Papers* September 1916

When Collett wrote in October 1912 that, 'the approach of winter is openly foreshadowed by the rapidly-decreasing daylight, the touches of frost, the falling of the leaf and the withering of the flowers', he was referring to his anticipation of winter pastimes; he could not realise how poignant such words might sound within a few years when the First World War had blighted a whole generation. Through the *Parish Papers*, and his use of them as a vehicle to spread news, he gives us a valuable picture, not only of the effects of war on a small village, but of the varying fortunes of a generation wrenched from its deep rural roots and thrust into a hostile world that stretched far wider than the trenches of Flanders. Indeed, for such a small community, it is surprising to find that it had representatives fighting in every service and just about every theatre of war.

The village, of course, had its share of regular soldiers who, through choice or pressures of limited employment, had enlisted earlier. One such was Percy George who came like many others from the Waifs and Strays Society to work as a kitchen boy at the vicarage. Enlisting in the 2nd Wilts during the spring of 1912, he sailed with his regiment to Gibraltar with two other village lads, Charlie Munday and Reggie Lewis. From here he wrote:

> We have been holding a siege here. We get stationed in groups on the rock to defend, while the fleet attack from the harbour. We have got a pretty good choir and had a photo taken in cassocks and surplices. I am getting on well here in the church. The King is coming in June.
> *Parish Papers* 4 June 1913

These halcyon days were not to last and when the war commenced Percy, by now at the front, was one of the first to be captured. Collett, not having heard from him since the war commenced, persistently badgered the War Office into providing information – a task he took up many times on behalf of village families. Eventually he discovered that Percy had become a prisoner of war at Gottingen, a captivity he was to endure until the end of hostilities.

In the village the effects of the war came slowly with merely a passing note in the Broadsheet:

> THE CONTINENTAL WAR – which has unfortunately broken out and may possibly affect our own country is very greatly to be deplored. Whatever the cause of it may be the inevitable consequence cannot fail to be bloodshed and misery for many. It is true that a nation's honour must be upheld but surely that might be accomplished without the loss of life. May God protect our land and save us from all peril and disaster.
>
> *Parish Papers* 5 August 1914

The day after war was declared the Prince of Wales' National Relief Fund was set up to help war sufferers and the villagers gave readily. The harvest proceeded steadily disturbed only by the noonday war bell when those who could attend were called every working day to a five-minute service. But a steady trickle of recruits were beginning to enlist. Miss Aldwynckle gave notice that her working party of village girls would commence their autumn tasks by preparing items for soldiers at the war and John Linnell, now enjoying a lusty middle age, started a small company of boy scouts whose first task was to canvass the parish for gifts of fruit and vegetables for the wounded soldiers convalescing in improvised quarters at Salisbury Workhouse. From the army camp at Fovant an increasing number of young soldiers made their way across the downs to find a welcome in the village homes. Mrs Greta Case, who had just left school to go into service with the Hardings, remembers her initial feelings of fear as the troops marched through the village with their horses and gun carriages as part of their military exercises, although such activities soon became accepted.

The first intimations of the more sinister effects of war came, not from France but, strangely, from America where Miss Giles, a parishioner, had travelled in the previous year. Her voyage to San Francisco had been much against the inclinations of the vicar who had tried to dissuade her because of the terrible earthquake of 1906 but Miss Giles was obviously made of sterner stuff. Her journey home on the *Franconia* from New York, however, provided as much excitement as she might have wished for:

> The *Franconia* left New York on November 2nd. We had then to go to St Johns Newfoundland to bring over 306 naval reserves. We got there later than

Henry Jay, 1886

expected and had to stay all night the men coming on board at six the next morning. The boat was painted black and grey, no flag flying and when it began to get dark the portholes were all covered so that she was in darkness outside. She carried a heavy cargo of lead for bullets. One man was caught signalling in the 3rd class cabin so they put him in irons. A steward left a porthole uncovered one night so lost his work. Everyone had to pass through an examination as to birth and whereabouts. At Liverpool it was more than one hour before we were landed, the tide driving us backwards and forwards. They said such a thing had never happened before. Such cheering you never heard, as went up when we were fairly started. Best wishes to all at Bowerchalke.

Parish Papers 9 December 1914

King George V directed that 3 January 1915 should be a day of Solemn Intercession for the war, a day when Bowerchalke joined its prayerful thoughts with the rest of the Empire; but life continued to be little ruffled by the terrible events across the Channel. Collett distributed his annual *Almanack* to all parishioners, the death occurred of Laura Freeth, for many years one of the village's most generous benefactors and fire destroyed a row of thatched cottages along the valley road. A further death, that of the Postmistress, Sarah Jane Habgood, and the collapse of her brother's carrier business which had been a pivot of the village economy for so long were of much more immediate concern. Only the schoolchildren's collection for the Belgian refugee children housed at nearby Sixpenny Handley was a reminder of the sufferings elsewhere.

In May came news of the first fatality. Private Isaac Sheppard of the 1st Battalion Coldstream Guards was killed in action at Richebourg, Belgium. 'Ikey', as he was known, a farm labourer from Misselfore, was the only fit one in his family, his two brothers suffering from the 'King's evil', a form of foot rot with progressively debilitating effects. Old Sally, his mother, had had a difficult job bringing them up as their father died very young.

In the same month a fund was set up to provide comforts for the men of the Wilts Regiment fighting at the front or being held prisoner of war. Parcels were collected every week and forwarded to the Regimental Depôt at Devizes. From there the Red Cross was able to route them to prisoners such as Percy George and other young villagers in captivity to whom the parcels from home (each with a *Parish Paper* from the vicar), represented the one bright moment in an otherwise monotonous existence. A postcard from Percy in August 1915, which was four weeks on the road stated:

> Am writing to thank you very much indeed for the books. Also your kind letter. The things I want very much are shirts and socks as I have only one pair of each at present. And I should like any kind of tinned food which you could send me.

The village responded immediately, several parcels arriving at the vicar's door within days of the news being printed.

Other young villagers were scattered among the camps of England preparing to replace the ever-increasing list of casualties from the front. Walter Coombs, a young chorister, was at the veterinary stables at Romsey while his brother Bertie was at Sutton Veny with the Hampshire Regiment where he described conditions in an army camp:

> We are in huts here which are fine for this lovely weather but when it is cold you find it. We have been working very hard lately as the whole Division is here and all 16 battalions work together once a week. We marched here from Bath – 24 miles – and it was a boiling hot day and it nearly killed us.
>
> *Parish Papers* 2 June 1915

Despite the difficulty of obtaining suitable labour the harvest was gathered in good time. There was no shortage either at the annual Harvest Festival with its usual generous offerings of corn, grapes, fruit and flowers. Sixty-three communicants attended, a sprinkling of military uniforms giving evidence of the changing times. Due to a decrease in the number of pupils, Wiltshire Education Committee had decided that the headteacher in future should be a mistress instead of a master. Thomas Penfound had, therefore, reluctantly handed in his resignation, married Priscilla Aldwynckle by special licence and departed for another position in Newbury – a further indication that war was beginning to cause movement to and from this previously static community on an altogether unprecedented scale. Almost daily old friends were departing and newer ones began to arrive. In came Mrs Hardwick from Bristol as the new headmistress to be near her husband, an army officer stationed at Salisbury; in came the Revd Stanley Bishop, Military Chaplain at the front and son-in-law to Henry Butler at Rookhaye; out went Cecil Finn, another deprived child reared for five and a half years at the vicarage who described his rude introduction to army life at Bovington:

> We had a very heavy day last Thursday. We were marching about all day at drill: when it was over the captain came round for men to run in a battalion cross country race. I went in for it and came in 16 out of 50 runners. When we got back before we could have any tea we had to fall in for a night's march. We walked 4 or 5 miles over the hill in the dark. We had not been in bed more than an hour when the bugle sounded the fire alarm. So out we tumbled in two ticks and fell into line with only our trousers and socks on. They kept us out in the cold for an hour and then told us to go back to bed: it was a false alarm. The next day we went for a long route march with full pack on. I can tell you we were about knocked out at the end.
>
> *Parish Papers* 10 November 1915

In October 1915 a public meeting was held in the schoolroom organised by the South Wilts Division of the National Emergency Campaign. Well-known speakers of different political parties addressed the villagers on how they could best help their country. Rather condescendingly, women were invited. Later, when their true value had at last been recognised, the invitation was to be somewhat warmer. The Bishop of Salisbury commenced a campaign to bring home, through a series of missions in each town and village in his diocese, the spiritual lessons of the war so that all might be uplifted to a higher and more noble life, thus enabling the troops to return to a country purified and improved. One wonders how these noble aspirations might have struck Robin Harding, now a young lieutenant in the thick of it:

> We had a simply terrific bombardment which lasted the whole of one night. The infantry went forward, our division was right in front and had a very hot time. The congestion on the roads behind the lines was beyond imagination. I had 1½ hours sleep that night in the back of the car. The villages behind the firing line are a sight, the wounded wandering about and lying against the wall all along the pavements. We went up and took about 800 back to a base

hospital the other day in our lorries. The natives here seem to carry on their work as usual just behind the firing line.

Parish Papers 18 October 1915

A new flag day, sponsored by Lady Pembroke, was announced in October to support the work of the Red Cross at the front, these were little buttonhole flags which the boy scouts sold at a penny each. On Trafalgar Day the Union Jack fluttered proudly from its mast in the schoolyard, while in France twenty year-old Arthur Lush of the Coldstream Guards died of his wounds in a hospital at Rouen. Collett commented:

By the death of Arthur Lush we are again reminded of the awfulness and terror of war. His is the third young life that has been sacrificed from our own parish and although they have been nobly and generously offered in the defence of their king and native land yet their withdrawal from their homes is a trial too great for description.

Parish Papers 17 November 1915

Arthur, son of the under-shepherd to Williamson, had been the best marksman in the village Rifle Club. When he left school he had worked for John Dimmer, a village grocer, for a while and then moved to the bakery at

Traction engine belonging to K&W.H. Stevens, Broadchalke, 1885

Gussage All Saints. A postcard from here to his mother shows him standing proudly outside the Gussage shop in his apron with the master baker. The message said:

> Dear Mother, I shall be home on Saturday night if nothing to stop me as I am going to try to get baker in the army for the War. I think we must all try now the War is on.

After his death, his mother at her cottage at Buddens, received a letter from the sister who had nursed him at Rouen:

> . . . He was most wonderfully bright and cheerful and sent his love to you. He was almost unconscious all night and up to his end so sent no messages. He did not suffer much and his end was peace. Matron always provides flowers and I tie them with ribbon and put them on the coffins. . . .

Jack Burton had been the proud driver of the village motorbus. Provided by Robert Williamson, it was split into two with the front half for passengers and the rear for milk churns and painted conspicuously in what the *Salisbury Journal* described as 'red lake'. With the call-up of his driver, and the scarcity of replacement labour, Williamson sold the bus to a new proprietor at Bishopstone and Jack Burton, soon stationed behind the front line in France, was homesick for his feather bed. Sleeping in lorries under constant barrage with cats and rats for company, he was grateful for the *Parish Papers* to keep him in touch with normality. Back home the contrast was stark. His past employer was preparing for the marriage of his daughter, Lettie, the social event of the year. It was a glorious day in late November and by 1 o'clock the village was astir with motor cars and carriages blocking the road from Salisbury. The bridal party was met at the church door by the vicar while John Linnell played rousing wedding marches and the bells pealed out merrily. A reception was held for one hundred guests at Knowle Farm and during the evening a large number of parishioners and friends were invited to supper. For a while the war was forgotten, but in the following week came the official acknowledgement of the death of the first of the two Whitehead brothers to die in the war. George, another Coldstream guardsman, and an ex-farm labourer with a reputation at school for a quick temper, had been missing for almost a year but a slender hope of his survival had remained until the official notice was received.

Christmas that year was spent very quietly in Bowerchalke. Beautiful white chrysanthemums decked the church altar but the festivities of previous years were muted. From the front, Bert Burton was writing: 'It has been very rough this Christmas but we had a very good time. The army chaplain is very good and the officers got up concerts for the troops to pass the time when they are resting.' George Foyle, who had recently joined the Royal Navy, was worrying rather belatedly from HMS *Impregnable* at Devonport that he could not swim. In Gibraltar Jesse Jackson, ex-vicarage boy and gunner in the Royal Artillery, was bemoaning his remoteness from the action.

Already tales of heroism were filtering home. Charlie Case, son of a carter in Quidham Street, was a submariner, a regular seaman. Submarines were a new and untried weapon at this time, often as dangerous to its crew as to the enemy. Charlie was serving in one of a small number of submarines that went through the minefields of the narrow Dardanelles Straits to attack Turkish bases in the Sea of Marmora. For this he received the DSM. A member of the Harding family, Herbert Cowl acting as Chaplain to the Forces, had been badly wounded in the jaw and sent home on the ill-fated *Anglia* when it was torpedoed. He was blown out of his bunk into the passageway and crushed between the wreckage. A wave washed him free and he managed to get on deck where he insisted on helping to rescue those with worse wounds than himself and went down with the boat. Being an excellent swimmer he managed to reach a raft from whence he was eventually picked up and conveyed to a hospital in England.

The darkest days of the war in 1916 saw Kitchener's army beginning to play an increasingly major part. The school was to lose its best teacher early that year. Ellen Whitcomb from the Infants' Department had given fourteen years excellent service but the continuing decrease in the number of pupils forced the Education Committee to reduce staff. Ironically as soon as she left the numbers started to rise again which was most satisfactory from the point of view of grants but made life considerably harder for the headmistress and her remaining assistant. The winter Sunday school treat was held as usual in the schoolroom, but a blackout was imposed on all houses and churches an hour and half after sunset forcing Collett to begin Evensong earlier. Church bells, too, were forbidden from tolling after dark and even the church clock prevented from striking the hour, all grim reminders that military attack from the air, for the first time in history, was always a possibility.

On Thursday 1 March a day of Solemn Intercession, the Revd Tupper Carey, once rural dean and now Canon of York Cathedral, addressed a series of packed services in impressive and inspiring tones stating that the war was the punishment due to all for past indifferences and irreligious neglect of God – grim prophecies given further credence, it must have seemed, by a snowstorm which continued for several days practically cutting the village off and causing the postponement of the schoolchildren's fund-raising play 'Dame Durden's Shoe'.

With labour beginning to get desperately short as more and more young men left the valley Lady Pembroke issued an appeal to the women of

C. Maidmont with his cart, September 1888

Wiltshire to assist in the cultivation of the land. Help would be required in every department of farming activity: milking, clearing the land, ploughing, haymaking, harvesting, poultry and bee-keeping as well as the vital need to cultivate vegetables. Every house was approached to find out who could help and to advise on hours of employment and rates of pay. For the first time women were made to feel they had a vital role to play outside the home, a movement which was to prove a far more powerful factor for them than years of suffragette agitation.

Food was desperately needed not just for the home market but for the vast military machine encamped in England and France and the local agent, Edward Bailey at Broadchalke, bought up every available vegetable for army supplies. Schedules were also sent out to farmers asking them to give particulars of any surplus hay and straw so that the huge numbers of horses could be cared for properly. To allow longer hours in the fields the Daylight Saving Bill was passed which seemed to Collett the legal enforcement of a lie: 'for if by law we are to put our clocks on an hour it will not convince any sensible person that it is 7 o'clock when they know very well it is only six!'

News was also arriving of activities in more remote theatres of war. Three young soldiers of the Yorkshire Regiment, who had always found a welcome in the home of Mrs Golden in Quidham Street, wrote of their eventful journey to Egypt, colliding with a French boat near Malta and being fired at by a submarine after leaving Alexandria. At Port Said the weather was intensely hot making them yearn for the refreshing breezes of the Chalke valley. Norman Butler, whose mother ran a private school for farmers' sons in the village, was also in Egypt where he was injured in the shoulder by enemy fire. In Salonica, Fred Harte from Woodyates was finding the weather very different. After leaving France his regiment suffered a stormy voyage before landing in deep snow followed by two days' miserable rain with only canvas tents for shelter.

In Bowerchalke the spring blossom and flowers were transforming the countryside as they do each year, the air heavy with scent, and the rapid movements of returning swallows forced the vicar to close the church doors to prevent them nesting in the porch. An excited audience was entertained in the schoolroom by the 1st Battalion Victoria Rifles and on Empire Day the children assembled once more in the yard to salute the flag, sing the National Anthem and give their pennies for the 'Empire Day gift from British boys and girls to the brave fighting forces'. Also, as usual, they scoured the hedgerows for sedges and wild flowers for the annual Hay Harvest. In May Clem Vincent, whose next door neighbour, Isaac Sheppard, had been the first to fall, was killed in action with the Persian Expeditionary Force having already been wounded on two previous occasions. Fred Penny remembers the Vincents well: 'Clem's family had a smallholding at Misselfore with a few cows and a few horses and did a bit of contract work carrying flints for road making for the Council.' Greta Case also remembers him in the days before he joined the Wiltshire Regiment as a regular soldier, helping his father take the cows up to Poor Patch where he stayed all day to make sure they did not stray.

Bertie Goodfellow was to die with Lord Kitchener. His father was the Baptist colporteur, travelling the villages in his donkey cart distributing religious literature for Spurgeon, the great revivalist from the London Metropolitan Tabernacle. Bertie was a quiet lad, the elder of two sons, he served on the armoured cruiser *Hampshire* in the modest capacity of cook's mate. In early June while conveying the Secretary of State for War on an official mission to Russia, the ship struck a German mine off the west coast of the Orkneys. There was a strong gale and 15 minutes later the *Hampshire* went down with very few survivors.

Walter Coombs was the next to die. His family lived at Binghams Cottages and his father drove Robert Williamson's van filled with the neatly-tied bunches of watercress into Wilton each day for the London train. Walter and his brother Bertie, stationed in Salonica, had also worked for the Williamsons and were two of the village's best choristers. A private in the Hampshire Regiment, Walter was hit by a shell and killed instantly. Two weeks later, Tom Anderson, 'a fine, tall and healthy lad of nineteen' also died in the excessive heat of Basra, Mesopotamia.

Not all the news was quite so grim. George Jenkins, well-known in the village as the baker's boy from the general stores in Broadchalke, was with the Devons stationed with a cyclists' company in Suffolk. Camped right on the sea coast, their job was to guard against Zeppelins, although it is difficult to see what they could do about them as anti-aircraft defence at that time was inadequate. One evening they had the call to turn out of camp and after marching for two hours lay helplessly in a hedge as they watched three Zeppelins drop bombs on the shore less than a mile away.

One of the many grateful recipients of the *Parish Papers* was a Colonel Cooke in command of the 9th Welsh Regiment who had visited Bowerchalke regularly with his family when living at the Old Rectory in Broadchalke. After thirteen months in France he had seen a considerable amount of the war but wrote to say his battalion was still a very fine one with 'good discipline – good heart'. His regimental motto of 'death rather than dishonour' he supplemented with another: 'always merry and bright'. His men must have needed this sort of encouragement as they passed through all the heavy fighting of that time losing twelve officers and five hundred men. In one of his letters to Collett he remarked:

> I am proud of my command. I have had very good health and very good luck. The strain has been great, the anxiety immense. Remember me to any friends at Broadchalke and Bowerchalke. . . . I receive the Parish Paper and always like reading it. It is such a helpful little paper and I like to read the news of the place reminding me of the pleasant time I spent at Bowerchalke.
>
> *Parish Papers* 23 August 1916

Hedley Hardiman, son of the blacksmith and Arnold Hardwick, the schoolmistress's son, were among several reported wounded at that time and in early October the second of the Whitehead brothers from Quidham Street, William, died only sixteen weeks after his marriage in the parish church. Second Lieutenant Usher, his Platoon Commander in the 1st Wilts wrote:

> Pte Whitehead was in my own platoon and was one of the best men I had, always the keenest of soldiers. He was hit in the head by a German sniper and luckily suffered no pain, as he never recovered consciousness and died very shortly after being hit. His death was deeply regretted by us all he being a great favourite among the men and officers.
>
> *Parish Papers* 1 November 1916

The gloom caused by such news at home was reinforced by violent November storms with torrential rain and strong gales bringing down trees and blocking roads. Transport was proving difficult anyway with the valley bus proving to be increasingly unreliable. Mechanical trouble, hindered by lack of spares and the sickness of the driver, put it out of action for weeks at a time leaving Harding's milk motor as an uncomfortable alternative each Tuesday. It was at this time that Henrietta Soffe, shopkeeper and seamstress at Woodminton for many years, finally died peacefully in her bed aged ninety. Only the children's Christmas concert in a schoolroom decked with flags and evergreens appears to have raised their spirits at that time, although early in the New Year a police order did allow the bells to be rung and clocks struck up to 9 o'clock at night.

Food supplies were becoming increasingly difficult in 1917. By February potatoes were scarce and those that had been kept for planting had been blighted by the hard frosts. Bread was also a cause for concern; so much so that in May a royal proclamation was read out during church services urging the necessity of using it as economically as possible. Appeals were made for Englishmen to forego their Sabbath rest to further cultivate the land. Fred Penny, whose father kept the largest of the village stores, remembers the expectancy in the air when the supplies van of George Page and Sons from Southampton paid their fortnightly visit. The cry would rapidly go around 'Pages have come!', but often their supplies were very meagre and William Penny had a difficult job convincing some villagers that his distribution was an equitable one.

The condition of those who were prisoners of war was also worrying. By this time seven hundred Wiltshire servicemen were in enemy hands, among them Percy George, recently moved from Gottingen to another camp in Cassel, suffering severely from bronchitis. Collett urged the village to a greater effort for the prisoners of war and John Linnell was despatched on a house-to-house collection which raised over £25. Meanwhile Frank Morris, son of the village pig slaughterer from Misselfore, left to join his five brothers in the army. Although none of them were killed, three had been wounded and returned to England for recuperation while Frank was gassed early the following year. Further losses were recorded: Private Martin Chubb of the Welsh Fusiliers aged thirty-eight, killed in France; Harry Stagg, aged twenty-seven, whose wife Leila had already lost her brother, Clem Vincent, and was now left with two small children. Private Claud Compton was seriously wounded in action, and Lieutenant Harris, recently married into the Butler family was also badly wounded.

Although Hedley Golden is recorded as being killed in action on 4 October 1917 it was a long time before his family received any official confirmation. A quiet, serious-minded boy, his sister Kate Gulliver recalls that his entry into the services had been delayed because of his work on their Middle Chase Farm. In September 1916, however, he joined the Royal Artillery but was transferred to the King's Own Yorkshire Light Infantry which had suffered severe losses. He obtained leave at Christmas when his family saw him for the last time. In February he was sent to France to join the terrible Ypres offensives. In early October, all contact with him ceased and it was Edward Collett who once more pressurised the War Office for information. In mid-November Hedley was officially listed as missing, presumed killed, at Passchendaele. Collett continued with his enquiries but it was not until eight months later that any definite evidence of his fate was forthcoming. Through the Red Cross, a young Yorkshireman was traced, a Private Harbury, who was able to report, 'I was near Ypres in the Passchendaele Sector trying to drive back the Germans on October 4 1917. I went over the top the same time as Golden and saw him killed outright. He was buried near but there was no time for a burial service'. Hedley was another chorister, described by Collett as 'a lad of great promise, faithful and reliable'. It is impossible to imagine the horrors experienced by a young man of sensitive nature taken from such a rustic backwater as the Chase and thrust like so many thousands of others into the worst holocaust the world had ever known, a thought perhaps not lost on the mourners when later that month the Bishop of Salisbury requested that all church bells should be rung to commemorate the great victory won in France.

Increasing austerity at home, continued bleak reports from the Front, no wonder people were ready to grasp desperately for any grain of comfort:

> VISIONS OF ANGELS – have been recently granted in different parts of England to the astonishment of the beholders. There are some who think that such manifestations are mere fancy. But there is no ground for doubt. Angels have *always* been God's messengers to men. While we must reject superstition we dare not refuse revelation.
>
> *Parish Papers* 19 September 1917

Despite Collett's readiness to anticipate divine intervention, within the village he gave his support to more practical measures. A nurse was at last appointed to serve the needs of Bowerchalke and Broadchalke jointly and a representative of the Board of Agriculture gave demonstrations in potato-spraying to help all, even those with the tiniest plot of land, to improve their output. War Savings Cards obtainable from the Post Office enabled villagers to purchase sixpenny stamps towards a 15*s*. 6*d*. war certificate with interest paid at 1*s*. a year, thus helping the country as well as themselves. A limited amount of sugar was made available to those cottagers prepared to make jam, an activity eagerly subscribed to by the children who were granted time off from school to collect blackberries for jam to be sent to the troops abroad. On Saturday afternoons under the direction of their Sunday school teacher, Nellie Goodfellow, a group continued to meet and make little garments and picture books for the 'poor orphan infants of the many brave soldiers who had fallen in the war', and the Christmas Concert, under the direction of their new headmistress, Bessie Wilson, raised £2 15*s*. 0*d*. for the Red Cross Fund.

The terrible battles in Europe were to continue for much of 1918, but in England, Charlie Case, now a Chief Petty Officer in the submarine service

Sidney Williams, the carrier's son with 'Coco' and carriage, 10 September 1888

was to die in very tragic circumstances. His sister-in-law, Greta Case, remembers Charlie's ambition to join up when he was still a boy. His father was head carter on Shrewsbury Harding's farm and Charlie started work there on leaving school, but soon found the life tedious. One day, while leading two horses with another young labourer, they both decided to leave. Tying the horses to a hedge they ran away to join the army. The other boy passed but Charlie was rejected because of his youth and returned home to face the music. Later, however, he persuaded his father to allow him to join the boy's section of the navy and later still joined the submarine service where in 1915 he had received the DSM. By 1918, now aged thirty-eight and with a wife and three young sons in Portsmouth, Charlie Case had served a long and dangerous war. The end of January brought to a close the British submarine service's blackest month since the beginning of the war, and with it, his career came to an end.

Operation EC1 was a cruiser exercise involving almost the entire Grand Fleet. Charlie Case was in submarine K4, one of eight of this type involved in the exercise. The steam-driven 'K' boats had a disastrous history having been involved in a number of unfortunate incidents since their inception in 1916. In darkness the line of ships emerged from the Forth Estuary when a group of minesweeping trawlers, ignorant of the fleet operation in progress, steamed across the line. In the ensuing chaos several submarines were wrecked and K4 was hit broadside on by her sister vessel K6. Although K6 managed to tear herself free, K4 sank so rapidly that another vessel arriving within seconds directly in her path passed right over the spot where she had vanished without even scraping her keel. It was a chaotic situation in which the escorting destroyers ploughed right through the survivors in the water cutting them to pieces with their propellers and by the time they had passed clear only nine men remained alive. None were from K4.

According to Greta Case, Charlie had been overdue for retirement but had been involved in this exercise because of his experience. His wife found herself unable to bring up her sons on her own and they were sent away to a naval school. Later, however, they left England with her to start a new life on an Australian sheep farm.

The scarcity of paper in the latter part of the war threatened the existence of the *Parish Papers* which through its continued news of home was proving to be a valuable aid to morale in all theatres of war where Bowerchalke families were represented. Food supplies, however, continued to be the most desperate need – especially potatoes. 'Under war conditions', urged Prime Minister Lloyd George, 'there is no crop which can compete with it in importance as a food for either man or beast.' The spring sowing of that year, therefore, was of inestimable importance and Charles Elliott, Chairman of the Parish Council, called a public meeting to seek ways of increasing this vital crop still further. Rationing was introduced at last, an event which brought a rare moment of humour from Collett in those troubled times:

> RAS*IONS! – of all the extraordinary and unforeseen results of the war, the previous mispronunciation of the word RATION is the most laughably ridiculous. It sounds exactly as though there was an epidemic of sneezing when one hears everyone even educated people calling out for their Rash-ions. Anyhow so long as we are under the dark war cloud and we are depressed and sad there is no harm in having a joke about this peculiarity. The indig-nashun of all our nash-un will bring condemn-nashun upon such pronunci-ashun! Perhaps discrimi-nashun may bring an improvement and expla-nashun.
>
> *Parish Papers* 6 March 1918

With no end to the war in sight Bowerchalke was to lose two more of its bright young men. Fred Butler, son of the Methodist farmer from Rookhaye, joined the Royal Flying Corps and served in 65 Squadron at Swingate Down, Dover. He was a farmer born and bred whose greatest joy had been riding over the downs of the Chalke Valley. Flying was an art still in its infancy and on 22 April he wrote home:

> Today is quite fine but very bumpy, quite unpleasant in the air – I have done

> two hours today and am going to do another soon – three hours a day is quite enough but I have got to finish my training this month. Things look a good deal better in France – I wish it was all over and we could return home and start farming again.

Three days later he was seen coming out of the mist near Dover and finding he was too close to earth, pulled his machine up suddenly causing it to roll over then crashing into a field and killing him instantly. His funeral at Bowerchalke on 1 April was conducted by his brother-in law Stanley Bishop, a Chaplain of the Forces. Fred Penny remembers it as the first funeral he ever attended where mourners had discarded the heavy black clothing and trimmings of such an occasion. Flying was obviously the wrong element for the Butler family for, strangely, within a few weeks his cousin Howard was also killed by falling from an aircraft at Farnborough.

Golden by name and golden by nature – Frank Golden was a village favourite. Unlike his more serious cousin, Hedley, who had died at Passchendaele, he was lively and always ready for a joke. Greta Case describes him as one of the most amusing characters she had come across: 'When visitors arrived at the school, the schoolmaster would often call on him to perform. He would stand up and recite Wiltshire rhymes in the old dialect and have us in fits. The visitors were delighted to hear him.' At fourteen, he left school to commence service with Edward Collett's brother John, priest-in-charge of Teffont but was often in the village to bear messages or visit his mother. Called up at eighteen, he was very soon in France with the Royal Irish Rifles where he wrote of his appreciation of the Church Army huts and the comforts they provided for the troops. He died of wounds shortly after. The regard with which he was held was further illustrated by the Memorial Service held at Teffont and the twenty-line poem, still preserved, that John Collett wrote in his memory:

> Dear boy, he is gone; he has passed to his rest
> Away from life's turmoil – God saw it was best.
> So young, yet so brave, and respected by all
> He has sacrificed life at duty's stern call. . . .

The last death to be reported, (though not the last to die), was of Private Arthur Lawes of the 2nd Wilts Regiment who came originally from Coombe Bissett. Following his marriage to Ella Linda Trowbridge in 1915 he came to live in Quidham Street, although after enlisting they saw very little of each other. Arthur died in Flanders on 8 May 1918. His young widow returned with their baby Kenneth to live with her parents at Misselfore where she remained without re-marrying until her death sixty-one years later.

The 1918 summer saw a further tightening of belts. The second delivery of letters, fought for so hard in the village, had been discontinued earlier in the year and the *Parish Papers*, which for a long time had been running at a heavy loss, were under even more pressure:

> PRINTING PAPER is now very difficult to get. We are now using up our present supply and it is just possible we may not be able to secure another lot in time for next week's paper. But we will try.
>
> *Parish Papers* 20 November 1918

The scarcity of butter and margarine had led to the use of 'mock butter' in the village, consisting of milk sufficiently thickened with cornflour, very slightly sweetened and turned out in little pats like real butter – not so appetising perhaps but more desirable than dry war bread! Bread remained, however, the prime necessity, and Lloyd George once again delivered an impassioned plea to British womanhood to lend their youth and strength to gathering in the desperately-needed harvest.

The schoolchildren continued to play their part in the war effort, raising funds to provide cigarettes for the soldiers at the front, holding concerts in support of the Red Cross and even selling picture postcards and flags in aid of the blinded soldiers fund. Nutshells and fruit stones had to be collected, too, as they produced a special kind of charcoal for respirators to be used by troops facing gas attack.

The summer treat of 1918, splendidly arranged by the Elliotts at Woodminton Farm, with games in the meadows and a modest tea in the barn went on as usual. Paper windmills were all the fashion then amongst the children causing Collett to remark wryly that they twirled round prettily but ground no corn! The steam roller made its annual visit to patch up the roads. News from the various theatres of war was still not good: Edney Williams from the carrier's family had lost his left arm. William Habgood from the Bell and Albert Trowbridge both had bad leg wounds and Cecil Finn, one of the vicarage boys, was suffering deafness as a result of shell shock. Percy George had been moved from his prisoner of war camp in Germany and interned in Holland hopefully counting on being returned to England.

With the proclamation of an armistice in November one can sense a communal sigh of relief sweep through the village. The church bells rang for a long period and Collett conducted a special thanksgiving service for a crowded congregation. There was no sudden, dramatic return to normality. How could there be after so much dislocation and human misery. A sense of numbness remained so that in March 1919 Collett, whose own health had been declining since the war's end, remarked: 'The sting of the war is still being very painfully felt both at home and abroad and a great sense of unrestfulness prevails everywhere in spite of the ending of the activities of open battle.' Gradually the sons of the village were demobilised, some to seek employment and continue their lives elsewhere. Lieutenant Charles Butler returned to Rookhaye after four and a half years from a war that had taken him to India, Mesopotamia, Persia and Southern Russia before making his way back home through the Dardanelles, Italy and France. Wilfred Penny was less fortunate. Having returned unscathed from the navy he broke his ankle in an accident and was conveyed to the Salisbury Infirmary!

For a long time nothing was heard of Percy George, the only one of the villagers to be a prisoner for the duration of the war, but in July came news. Following his release from the Germans he had been hospitalised for a long time with the recurrence of a high fever. His description of this and the experiences that led up to it give an interesting insight into the privations suffered by some prisoners at that time:

> I have been admitted to hospital again with a relapse of my old complaint of 1915. I was carried in with a temperature of 105 which is as high as a man can possibly live with and my pulse was at 112. I am much better now and improving rapidly. I have never before been able to tell you of my first experience of this fever but I will do so now. I was sent away to work in a quarry where we were at it ten hours a day digging out rock and wheeling it away to the factory. We had scarcely any food and very little clothing. It happened one morning early in December the sentry ordered me to follow him and took me to the top of a very high hill and made me stand without hat, boots or overcoat in a very fierce snow storm. I was in a shivering state of collapse. When the other Englishmen heard about me they refused to work until I was brought down and so I was fetched after four hours on the hill. I had to continue work in my wet clothes till night. Next morning I could hardly move and had lost my voice entirely. For several days I was not allowed to have a doctor and did not regain my voice for over a month. Since then I have been subject to sudden attacks of fever. . . .
>
> *Parish Papers* 27 August 1919

On his return to health he continued service with the Rhine Army but was hoping to re-visit the village on his next leave.

The day appointed by George V for national rejoicing was Saturday 19 July but excited preparations had been in hand since April. As so often in the past Manor Farm was to be the venue for a fête followed by a cricket match between married and single. At 4 o'clock there would be a free tea for all the children (cups must be brought), with a public tea for the rest at 5 o'clock. Various sports and dancing would take place during the evening with John Linnell, the secretary, appealing for helpers towards a scratch band. The flagpole, felled by a fierce gale two years earlier, was set up again and re-painted in order to hoist the flag. Unfortunately, the weather was not

Mr Butler's traction engine and thrashing machine at work, 27 August 1887

kind. The gaily-coloured decorations fluttered forlornly in heavy rain, the teas took place under the shelter of a barn and it was something of an anticlimax that all the sports had to be postponed until the following Saturday.

In September 1919 servicemen were still drifting back to their families. Harry Penny, badly wounded after four years of war, was finally well enough to return; William Habgood arrived from the Middle East even later in October. In November the School Log Book records that the headmistress, Mrs Wilson, was given a day off to meet her husband at Southampton. It was a particularly proud homecoming for RSM Wilson as he had recently received a meritorious service medal for his excellent management of the Arab labour corps at Basra.

It would seem that RSM Wilson was the last to return. What hopes any of them had for the future can only be conjectured but life, hastened by the effects of war, was changing. Bowerchalke, small and remote though it was, would not prove immune to such changes.

8
Widening Horizons

> We are glad to hear of the safe arrival in Australia of Mrs Woollett formerly Miss Margery Foyle and her husband. They had safe and pleasant passage and reached New South Wales last July. They are now living at a place called Newcastle where Mr Woollett who used to be in the Australian army has returned to his former employment in the Post Office.
>
> *Parish Papers* 17 September 1919

A long period of readjustment was to occur before peace in any meaningful sense of the word was to take place, a period of shortages, dislocation and grief was further hindered by a phenomenal rise in prices. Gradually, a degree of normality began to return. The bus, which had continued in a state of disrepair, appeared on the valley road again in June 1919 looking very attractive in its new coat of red paint and driven by its proud mechanic 'Captain' Jack Gulliver. The midday post, too, made a welcome return.

There had been little adult entertainment in the village apart from the occasional magic lantern lecture depicting scenes from the war, but in May 1920 Mr Cecil Barrie and his travelling company arrived to perform in the schoolroom to a large and appreciative audience who were glad to have something to smile about. The cricket team met to dust off its kit and reclaim a war-ravished pitch. Further down the valley at Bishopstone the Dowager Duchess of Pembroke opened a fête which had as its attractions a confetti battle and a baby show – the first of a rash of these – illustrating the effects of improved medical care and social legislation. Salisbury was blessed with magnificent weather that summer for its Great West of England Show which attracted huge crowds and kept the valley bus exceptionally busy over several days. The parties of London children recommenced their holiday visits and the schoolmistress, Mrs Wilson, gave birth, rather inconveniently, at the very beginning of the autumn term. Having continued its charities to help St Dunstan's Home for Blinded Soldiers and the re-building of the ruined homes of French peasants, the village paid tribute to its own dead with a marble plaque on the north wall of the church that November. Having honoured the fallen it now looked more hopefully to the future. The Christmas programme seemed to symbolise that intention with the church gaily decorated with flowers and evergreens and a programme of concerts and parties for both adults and children spread over several days.

The schoolroom, cramped and badly ventilated, had provided the only suitable accommodation for any village functions often to the inconvenience of the scholars. In 1921, however, a committee of ex-servicemen obtained one of the wooden huts from the old army camp at Fovant and erected it in Church Street. There appears to have been some disagreement about their intentions beforehand, so much so that ex-RSM Wilson, who had clearly taken a lead in the venture, felt compelled to issue a statement in the *Parish Papers*:

> THE RECREATION HUT – There apparently exists a doubt as to whether the hut is intended for an institution for ex-service men or a parochial building. To clear up this misunderstanding I wish to make it known that it was never the intention of the ex-service men to monopolise the room. On completion of the work, which will shortly be, a general parish meeting will take place when the present committee will formally hand over the room to be used as a village institute. It is hoped that all who are interested in making the room a success, will endeavour to attend.
>
> *Parish Papers* 26 October 1921

The hut was opened on 7 December with a whist drive and dance attended by well over a hundred villagers and friends. Between the two events, the vicar, now very frail, formally opened it for the use of the parish and wished it well in the future. The evening proved a great success marred only by the collapse of a rickety table containing all the crockery.

The new village hut, unhampered by the daily use of the children, was able to provide a much more convenient focal point for village activities. A Social Club was formed with a variety of games available as well as a regular round of dances, whist drives and dramatic entertainment. Despite this, village life was at the beginning of a new phase which was to change its character, gradually but irrevocably, from a largely self-sufficient community to a dormitory area for Salisbury and beyond.

The reasons for this change are complex but may be seen in the decline of rural life all over the country. At Bowerchalke, the First World War had given its younger generation glimpses of a wider society than the insular existence their forefathers had enjoyed. It is no wonder that many found it impossible to settle within the restricted range of opportunities available within a small village. The brief prosperity of the immediate post-war years gave way to a slump far worse than the Great Depression of the 1880s. In the early 1920s, with the repeal of the Corn Production Acts which had helped maintain prices, the 'drift from the land' gathered momentum as agricultural wages fell dramatically and workers were forced to turn to the towns. Nor were the women, whose broader capabilities had so ably stood the test of war, always ready to settle for rural domesticity. Two at least, Margery Foyle and Emily Gatehouse, married Australian soldiers previously stationed at Fovant and started new lives in New South Wales. Others started careers or marriages away from the cramped cottages of their families.

The sale of Pembroke estates in November 1918 had a profound effect on Bowerchalke and Collett's regret is clearly evident:

> The recent sales of lands and property which for many years have been owned by Lord Pembroke and his forefathers will mean great changes in our own parish as well as in all the neighbourhood. Among those who will so soon be leaving Bowerchalke are friends whom we shall miss more than we can tell and although others will take their place will never be forgotten.
>
> *Parish Papers* 3 September 1919

Among those farmers whose land was sold were two who had been there for the entire half-century of Collett's ministry. The Hardings from Manor Farm, the first to bring Fresian cattle into the valley and build up the famous 'Bowerchalke Herd', moved to Tarrant Rushden in Dorset. Charles Elliott, Chairman of the Parish Council and prime mover in many parish activities, left the Woodminton farm to retire to West Moors. The Michaelmas Flitchings in October 1919 saw the official changeover with cottagers departing who had lived in the village for many years; Frank Case, for example, who followed the Hardings to Dorset and continued with the family until his death recently at ninety-five. Others were able to take advantage of their tenure to buy their own property for the first time and rise in the social scale. Among these were Edward Hardiman the blacksmith, Edward Foyle the wheelwright and John Dimmer who purchased his little shop in Church Street.

The development of the internal combustion engine, with its effects on farm mechanisation and improved transport, was the most powerful influence in the decline of village life. Even before the war Robert Williamson's bus had brought Salisbury to within minutes of travel rather than hours. In October 1921 Mr Wort from Bishopstone, who had purchased Williamson's bus in 1915, replaced it with The Rambler, a more efficient vehicle providing a better service. It left Misselfore twice daily at 8 a.m. and 1 p.m. returning from the White Hart, Salisbury at 10 a.m. and 4 p.m. Shortly after, a Saturday service was added. Eventually the Wilts and Dorset Bus Company bought up the smaller one-man bus services in the Salisbury area to provide a vast county-wide complex. On the farm, the need for labour was progressively reduced as mechanisation took over more and more of the functions previously performed by men. Both these factors of improved transport and farm mechanisation led villagers to look further afield for employment, entertainment and accommodation.

As the century progressed and the Second World War led to further social change, the self-containment of the village collapsed as small local businesses, dependent on agricultural needs, either became obsolete or gave way to larger and more powerful competitors. Today, even the school, the Methodist Chapel and the Bell Inn have closed, only William Penny's store remains together with the Baptist and Anglican churches as reminders of the original community. Some of the old families are still represented: the Habgoods, the Hardimans and the Butlers to name a few, but overwhelmingly the inhabitants represent a new order of the wealthy retired, the 'second-homers', and those commuters fortunate enough to live in such a beautiful valley. The proportion of young people has dropped dramatically.

Edward Collett, of course, knew nothing of such trends. His health had begun to fail shortly after the First World War. Generous to a fault, such small resources as he had went to the production of his *Parish Papers* and charitable requirements, leaving very little for his everyday needs or the upkeep of the vicarage which was largely in the care of John Linnell. Mrs Monica Lee recalls the vicar in his latter years. When parochial responsibilities became too much for him, he would stay for a while with her father, Tom Habgood, a previous choirboy working in the Education Office at Plymouth. 'Robert Williamson would pay his train fare there,' she remembers, 'and my father would pay for the return journey.'

In 1921 there were a few short gaps in the weekly editions of the Broadsheet but he kept it going, continuing to send 170 copies to friends at home and abroad although the cost of postage had doubled in that year forcing him to send them off monthly. With the 1,703rd edition on 12 April 1922 production ceased abruptly with no explanation given. Two years later in May 1924, he died at the age of seventy-seven. The *Salisbury Journal* reported:

> We regret to announce the death of the Rev Edward Collett, vicar at Bowerchalke, which occurred on Wednesday night. Mr Collett, who had been 54 years in Holy Orders and vicar of Bowerchalke for 44 years, was greatly beloved by his parishioners for whom he lived a self sacrificing life. . . .

At his funeral, which took place in torrential rain, every house in the village was represented, his brother the Revd John Collett and John Linnell being the chief mourners. Thomas Penfound returned to play the organ and the Revd T.F. Forth, Collett's neighbour from Broadchalke, spoke of the three ideals that he always kept before him: the glory of God, a life of service for his flock and a life of prayer. His simplicity and dedication to the parish is better summed up by the Revd Francis Raikes, the Rector of Bishopstone, writing an obituary for the *Salisbury Diocesan Gazette*:

> When once he broke, some kind friends sent him some money to get away for a month's rest. He went, but the next week he was back again. He did all he could for the souls of his parishioners during the 46 years he was in charge. In the year 1879, (I) held a winter Mission in the parish, which had a lasting result. At its close the vicar said I shall have a Daily Celebration and from that day for 35 years he was to be found interceding for his people at the Altar. Often and often he was to be found on his knees in the quiet village church in prayer when no service was going on. . . .
>
> *Salisbury Diocesan Gazette* June 1924

Collett's grave, denoted by a plain tombstone, is to be found to the left of the church porch and a window at the west end of the nave is dedicated to his forty-six years of faithful service.

Appendix
Ghosts and Legends Concerning Bowerchalke

Stories of macabre happenings and ghostly encounters abound in Bowerchalke many of them passed down by word of mouth through the old village families, their validity is impossible to substantiate. The myth most likely to have basis in fact is the one quoted in Chapter 3 concerning a suicide in a well near the church. It was referred to by Kathleen Wiltshire in her *Ghosts and Legends of the Wiltshire Countryside*:

> Vernditch (near Bowerchalke) is the meeting point of the boundaries of Wiltshire, Dorset and Hampshire. Here, at the crossroads was said to be buried a suicide. Some say she was a girl from Bowerchalke, who drowned herself in a well near the churchyard; others that an old gipsy woman who used to frequent the Chalke Valley was found in the same well. As suicides were not buried in consecrated ground, she was interred here. An avenue of trees leads to the spot but they say no bird is ever heard to sing there.

It is the story of the gipsy woman known as Kit which is most quoted, giving her name to that three-county corner-stone of Vernditch known as 'Kit's Grave'.

The legends listed by Kathleen Wiltshire in her two books of county ghostlore were based on her investigations and interviews within the villages themselves. Here again they suffer, (but not in the telling!), from the difficulty of being several times removed. The following story, for example was told to her by a Mrs G. Daniel, who used to live in the Chalke Valley, and received the account from an elderly Bowerchalke resident recalling her youth:

> Mrs Daniel writes, (in her letter of 15 February 1975), that this old lady was supposed to be a witch, for she had cures for everything, made from herbs and flowers, which she picked from the fields. She also brewed her own beer, which was said to be delicious! When the old lady was a little girl, she and her family lived in a cottage (in Bowerchalke) which was all by itself in a field. On several occasions after they moved there they used to hear footsteps going round the outside of the house, but when her father went to the door there was no one to be seen.
>
> One winter's night, when there had been a heavy storm, they heard the footsteps again, so her father said he was going to see who kept going round the house but saw no one and there were no footsteps in the snow, which was piled up all round the walls. There is no explanation of this 'Happening'. The family lived in the cottage for years, and the footsteps continued to be heard, but no one was ever seen.

Field Barn is a possible location for this legend. It was in fact two cottages in the fields north of Rookhaye Farm which have now been demolished.

Pug's Hole, is a beautiful pastoral indentation in the downland south of Knowle Farm. Edith Olivier, the early twentieth century authoress from Wilton quotes the legend that a curious old thorn bush shaped like a garden seat grew here. On dark nights a voice could be heard crying pathetically, 'I'm lost! I want to go home,' but whenever a hunt was made the vision could be seen vanishing into the thorn bush. This area is called 'Shepherd's Bush' as the ghost is thought to be that of a poor shepherd who died there, allegedly in a snow drift.

This legend was one of a collection gathered together in 1956 during a period of furious investigative activity by the Bowerchalke Women's Institute. The following were also quoted by them and may have given rise to Bowerchalke's reputation as 'the most haunted village in Wiltshire'. It is interesting that the locations for these events are very widely spread:

Legend of the Downs – A golden coffin is buried somewhere on the Downs at Bowerchalke. It was stolen from one of the Briton's barrows. The theft was discovered and the coffin had to be hidden. At certain seasons seven men may be seen dragging the coffin over the Downs.

Patty's Bottom – A small valley between two hills at Woodminton. It is supposed to have been the scene of a great battle between the Romans and Ancient Britons. Legend relates that the valley was filled with blood. On certain moonlight nights tramping is distinctly heard and horses without heads can be seen rushing madly about.

Apple-spill Bridge – Legend tells that gold is hidden at the east end of the village. At a certain hour every night the ghost of a man with a lantern is seen. He follows pedestrians for a certain distance, rattling gold coins in a bag and clanking chains. If anyone could follow where the apparition leads, they would, of course, discover the treasure.

Sheppards Cross – Near the Post Office marks the spot where men were hung for sheep and deer stealing. The bodies were placed in an iron cage and left swinging as a warning to other miscreants. Descendants of an old lady called Chalke, tell the story of her sitting over the iron pot containing the Venison which was cooking to hide it from the Sheriff's Officers.

Verne Ditch – Legend tells that at a certain hour every night three distinct 'chops' can be heard. A large house called 'Lodge' once stood on this site (the cellars and walls of which still remain). The owner was found murdered, and the noise is supposed to be the sound of his head being chopped off.*

Some at least of these stories may have basis in fact – we shall never know. More convincing evidence of a Bowerchalke ghost, however, comes from Mrs Thelma Barter, a farmer's widow until recently living in quiet retirement in a house opposite the Woodminton farmhouse where she spent the greater part of her life. She is an intelligent and unemotional person who does not give the impression of being fanciful. Her story is fascinating:

> While I lived in the farmhouse I saw the ghost of an old lady several times. She was short, rather stout, and had a grey shawl round her shoulders. It was always in my bedroom that she appeared.

* Searches have been recently made, and no trace of the cellars and walls are to be found; according to W. Chafin, author of *Anecdotes Respecting Cranbourn Chase* the murder of the Lodge keeper took place in 1738.

In a nearby cottage called 'Craigleith' lived a very old blind lady, with a companion. Her name was Miss Elliott and she had been born at Woodminton. I went to see her one evening and described my ghost to her. She at once said it was her mother. Her companion found a very old photograph of Mrs Elliott and sure enough, it was my ghost.

When Timothy and Clare, as children, were ill, one night they both told me that someone had sat on the chair between the cots and held each child by the hand; they thought it was me, but I had not even been in their room during the night.

Some years after, I had moved to my present house and my son Richard, who continued to live in the farmhouse, came in for coffee. In the course of conversation, he asked me if I had seen an old lady upstairs in the farmhouse. He described my ghost as he had seen her. He said he had seen her several times. His poor wife, Susan, was terrified one morning as she vacuumed the bedrooms and someone spoke to her although no one was there! It was some time later before she finished the floor as she was too frightened to stay there. I had never spoken of the ghost to any of the children.

The 'baby sitter' for Richard also heard footsteps overhead, but found no one there except the children asleep in their beds. I spoke to old Mr Habgood about the strange happenings as he used to visit there as a child. He told me that Mrs Elliott was a very kind old lady and was very unhappy in the farmhouse.

I felt it important to include these accounts. Apart from the last one there is little, if any, factual basis for these tales, but within a stable rural community they would have some significance. The telling and re-telling, perhaps on winter evenings in primitive firelit cottages, would imprint themselves indelibly upon young, impressionable minds to form part of a mythology that would be impossible in 1985, with the transient nature of today's village dwellers.

Sources

Chapter 1
Parish Papers
Collett's Scrapbook, Vol. I
Salisbury Times 6 March 1882
Pamphlet: Report on a Village Conference, 1882
The Guardian 22 March 1882

Chapter 2
Parish Papers
Collett's Scrapbooks, Vols. I and II
Salisbury Times
Salisbury Mirror
Western Gazette

Chapter 3
Parish Registers (Bowerchalke Church and Wiltshire County Records Office)
1881 Census Return (Wiltshire County Records Office)
Kelly's Directories 1855–1915
Brown's Directory of Salisbury 1912
Bowerchalke Village Almanack 1883
Parish Papers
Salisbury and Winchester Journal 2 September 1822
History of Modern Wiltshire, Everard Arundell and Colt Hoare, 1829
Modern Wiltshire: Hundred of Chalke 1830
Victoria County History of Wiltshire, Vol. IV
Natural History of Wiltshire, Aubrey, 1847
Anecdotes and History of Cranborne Chase, William Chafin, 1818
A Chronicle of Cranborne and Cranborne Chase, T.W. Waite Smart, 1841
Cranborne Chase, Desmond Hawkins, 1980
Life in a Wiltshire Village, H. Poole, 1975
Women's Institute Scrapbook, 1956

Chapter 4
Return to Bishop of Salisbury's Visitation Queries 1783 and 1879 (Wiltshire County Records Office)
Parish Records (Bowerchalke Church and Wiltshire County Records Office)
Parish Papers
Collett's Scrapbooks, Vols. I, II and III
Salisbury Mirror and Express 15 July 1887
Research notes by Mrs Greta Adams (ex-Headmistress of Bowerchalke School)
Bowerchalke Women's Institute Village Diary 1956
Rural Life in Wessex, J.H. Bettey, 1977

Chapter 5
School Log Books 1875–1924 (Wiltshire County Records Office)
Census Return 1881 (Wiltshire County Records Office)
Return to Bishop of Salisbury's Visitation Queries 1879 (Wiltshire County Records Office)
Parish Papers Collett's Scrapbooks Vols. I, II and III
Research notes of Mrs Greta Adams (ex-Headmistress of Bowerchalke School)
The Children's Society Archives, Kennington Road, London

Chapter 6
Parish Papers
Collett's Scrapbook, Vol. II
Salisbury Express 3 August 1888
Salisbury Journal 4 August 1888

Chapter 7
Parish Papers
Collett's Scrapbook, Vol. IV
Daily Express 29 April 1918
Imperial War Museum, London
Commonwealth War Graves Register for Naval Personnel, the Portsmouth Memorial
'A Damned Un-English Weapon', *The Story of Submarine Warfare*, Edwyn Gray, 1971

Chapter 8
Schedule of Property Sales in relation to the Pembroke Estate, November 1918
Parish Papers
Salisbury Diocesan Gazette June 1924
Salisbury Journal 9 and 16 May 1924
Rural Life in Wessex, J.H. Bettey, 1977
Shell Book of Rural Britain, Keith Mossman, 1978

Appendix
Ghosts and Legends of the Wiltshire Countryside. K. Wiltshire, 1973
More Ghosts and Legends of the Wiltshire Countryside. K. Wiltshire, 1984
Bowerchalke Women's Institute Village Diary, 1956
Mrs Thelma Barter, Woodminton Cottages

Index

Accidents, 28, 39, 41–4, 99, 114
Aldin, Claud, 99
Aldwynckle, Priscilla, 11, 65–6, 67–8, 70, 72, 89–90, 92, 94, 107, 109, 113, 116
Allen, Revd Taprell, 51
Almanack, 50, 52, 114

Bazaars, 81, 103
Baby shows, 38, 131
Band of Mercy, 10, 66, 90
Baptist chapel, 30, 51–2
Baptists, 2, 3, 6, 7, 51, 52, 59, 80, 95–6
Barter, Thelma, 34, 139–40
Bell Inn, 29, 40, 128, 134
Blackout, 60, 119
Bodleian Library, 17
Bond, Emma Jane, 53
Bond, Sarah, 29
Boot Club, 66
Bowerchalke United Friendly Society, 4, 35, 46–9, 78, 86, 99, 100, 109
Bowerchalke WI, 139
Brass Band, 48, 66, 101, 109
Butler, Fred, 126–7
Butler, Henry, 25, 43, 116, 126

Caddy, James, 83–8, 101
Case, Charlie, 119, 124–6
Case, Greta, 48, 72, 87, 90, 113, 121, 125, 126
Case, William, 87, 111
Chase, the, 31, 41, 68, 73–5, 81, 82, 91, 97, 104, 124
Chubb, Martin, 123
Church; Army, 107–8, 127
 baptism, 7, 28, 59
 behaviour, 8, 60–3
 bells, 53, 54, 63, 119, 123, 124
 burials, 27–8, 53, 54, 62, 134
 choir, 3, 9, 53, 62, 66, 70–2
 clock, 4, 10, 21–2, 60, 119, 123
 fabric, 2, 3, 50, 53, 59, 60, 63, 103, 135
 marriage, 11, 15, 48, 64
 services, 2, 3, 4, 6, 51, 53–62, 66, 119, 123, 128, 135
 S.P.G., 59, 107
 Sunday school, 9, 66–70, 107, 119
 Times, the, 74–5
Clothing Club, 6, 35
Coal Club, 6, 35
Collett, Augustus, 1
 Harry, 1
 John, 1, 72, 107, 127
 John Homes, 1
 Sophia Eleanor, 1
Compton, Caroline, 66, 79, 80–3
Cooke, Colonel, 122
Coombs, Bertie, 112, 115, 121
 Ellen 35, 54, 65, 86, 101, 104, 105
 John, 47, 48, 65, 72, 104, 134
 Polly, 44–5
 Walter, 115, 121
Coronation, 48
Cowl, Herbert, 119
Cranborne Chase, 25, 27
Cruse, Sgt, 8

Dances, 102, 107, 129, 132
Daylight Bill, 60, 119, 120
Daily Chronicle, 12, 17
Daily Express, 15, 52
Daily Mirror, 12
Deveraux, Hugh, 97
Dimmer, John, 35, 103, 117, 133
Du Cann, Prof, 105–6
Dinah, Mr and Mrs, 105

Education Act 1891, 84
Education Act 1902, 85–6
Elliott, Charles, 31, 42, 68–9, 84, 105, 107, 126, 128, 133
 Jasper, 41, 63, 67
 John, 73
Emigration, 12, 19, 21, 28, 29, 44–5, 97–8
Empire Day, 81, 121
Entertainment, 86–7, 93–4, 100, 104–7, 108–9, 119, 121, 124, 131, 132, 133
Flower Show, 14, 81, 100, 101–3
Foote, George, 87, 106
Foyle, Augustus, 75
 Edward, 66
 family, 19, 96, 109, 110
 George, 119
 Margery, 131, 133
 Polly, 36
 Thomas, 29, 88
Freeth, Laura, 65, 67, 114
Furnice, Maria, 77, 78

Games and pastimes, 14, 70, 100, 109, 110, 111, 117, 128, 129, 131, 132
Gatehouse, Bill, 72, 108
George, Percy, 20, 112, 113, 115, 123, 128, 129
Giles, Miss, 113–4
Glee Club, 107
Goddard, P.c., 103
Golden, Frank, 72, 107, 127
 Hedley, 123–4
 Kate (later Gulliver), 44, 75, 91, 123
Goode, Harry, 27
Goodfellow, Bertie, 121
 Nellie, 94, 99, 109, 124
Gramophone, 67, 72, 108–9
Gramshaw, W.H., 102
Great West of England Show, 131
Greenstock, Harry, 44
Grove, Sir Thomas, 101
Guardian, The, 7
Gypsies, 45–6

Habgood, Eddie, 40, 58
 Isaac, 29
 Isaac (Junior) 40–1
 Tom, 110, 134
Hardiman, Edward, 29, 33, 79, 110, 133
Harding, Shrewsbury, 7, 83, 101, 110, 113, 125, 133
Hardwick, Mrs, 93, 116

Harvest Festival, 35, 54–5
Hay Harvest, 54–7, 121
Holiday children, 9, 94–6, 131
Hull Daily Mail, 15

Illness, 31–2, 35, 38, 46, 76, 77, 78, 91, 93
Industrial Exhibition, 103

Jubilee, 48
Jumble sales, 103

Kendall, William, 7, 79
Kerley, Thomas, 44
King's College, Cambridge, 28, 105
Kitchener, Lord, 119, 121
Kits Grave, 45, 138

Larmer Tree Gardens, 69–70
Lawes, Arthur, 127
Lea, Lady Herbert of, 50
Lee, Monica, 40, 134
Library, 6
Lilley, John and Mary, 24
Linnell, John, 1, 22, 45, 46, 66, 68, 70, 72, 75, 95, 96, 101, 106–7, 109, 110, 113, 118, 123, 129, 134
Lloyd George, 22, 126, 128
Lloyd, Thomas, 83
Longman, Dr, 35
Lush, Arthur, 111, 117–8
Lutt, Revd, 76

McAlpine, Robert, 78–9
Magic Lantern, 72, 86, 107–8, 131
Marleycombe Down, 109, 110, 139
Medical Club, 35, 36
Methodist chapel, 8, 51, 60, 134
Michaelmas Flitchings, 14, 28, 133
Moving pictures, 108
Muller, Inez, 75

National Insurance Act, 36, 48–9, 100
Newman, Raymond, 97, 99

Outdoor relief, 30

Pearce, William Bishop, 97, 99
Pembroke, Lady, 117, 119, 131
Pembroke, Lord, 14, 25, 27, 33, 35, 50, 73, 74, 75, 76, 100
Pembroke, sales, 133
Penfound, Thomas Hyde, 43, 88–92, 107, 116, 134
Penny, Charlie, 29
  Fred, 12, 29, 36, 40, 41, 111, 121, 123, 127
  James, 48
  Lizzie, 32, 81
  readings, 109
  William, 29, 123
Pig Club, 6, 33–4
Pitt-Rivers, General, 69
Poor Patch, 27, 121
Post Office, 6, 22, 38, 40, 41, 42, 139
Primrose League, 109

Rations, 126, 128
Recreation hut, 132

Sale of work, 66, 99, 103
Salisbury Fair, 111
Salisbury Infirmary, 35, 42, 54, 56, 65, 66, 109
Salisbury Journal, 8, 28, 73, 118, 134
Salisbury Mirror, 68–9
Salisbury Times, 12, 15, 16–17, 21, 47, 80, 99
Sanitation, 31–3, 76, 77, 93
Scrap sale, 103
School inspections, 76–86
  night, 83, 91
  teachers, 3, 7, 43, 73–94, 96–7, 101, 105, 107, 115–6, 119, 124, 127, 130, 131, 132, 134
  treats, 81–2, 86–7, 107, 128
Sheppard, 'Ikey', 115, 121
  Isaac, 4, 8, 48, 86
Smith, nurse, 36, 124
Smithers, nurse, 36, 93, 124
Social Club, 132
Soffe, Henrietta, 29, 35, 122–3
Soup kitchen, 6, 35
St Bartholomew's Orphanage, 9, 97
Stagg, Harry, 123
Stevens, Supt, 8
Stone, Sarah, 66
Swindon Advertiser, 62

Titanic, 44
Transport: bicycle, 36, 38, 43, 44, 107, 111, 122
  bus, 70, 89, 111, 118, 121, 122, 131, 133
  car, 38, 43, 72, 116, 133
  horses and waggons, 4, 9, 25, 28, 29, 30, 35, 38, 39, 40, 41–2, 46, 51, 55, 57, 63, 67, 68, 69, 75, 95
Tupper Carey, Revd, 119

Vestry meetings, 64
Village Club, 4, 35, 46–9, 78, 86, 99, 100, 109
Vincent, Clem, 121, 123

Waifs and Strays, 9, 90, 96–9, 103, 107, 112
Waite, Eliza, 79
Warren, Winnie, 105
Welch, Walter, 29, 35
Western Gazette, 16, 62
Whist drives, 132
Whitehead, George, 118
  William, 122
Wild West Show, 111
Wilkins, Jane (Senior), 73, 96
  Jane, 9, 73–5, 82, 96–7, 104, 105
  William, 6, 35, 64–5, 73
Williams, Ann, 53
  Anna, 40, 95
  Edney, 128
  Eliza, 97, 99
  Ernest, 40
  Josiah, 6, 28, 38, 40
  Revd Rowland, 50
  Sarah Jane (later Habgood), 38, 40, 42, 114
  Sydney, 40, 111
  William, 38, 39, 40, 42, 111, 114–5
Williamson, Robert, 25, 40, 47, 48, 70, 87, 89, 92, 101, 102, 107, 110, 118, 121, 133, 134
Wilson, Bessie, 93–4, 124, 130, 131
Wilson, RSM, 94, 130, 132
Wiltshire Arts and Crafts Association, 109
Wiltshire, Kathleen, 138
Wiltshire Musical Festival, 90
Wiltshire Nursing Association, 36
Witcombe, Ellen, 89, 92, 93, 119
Wood, Maria, 65, 66, 68, 72, 86
Wordsworth, Bishop John, 57, 83
Wyatt, T.H., 50